Francis Peloubet

Select songs

For the singing service in the prayer meeting and Sunday school

Francis Peloubet

Select songs
For the singing service in the prayer meeting and Sunday school

ISBN/EAN: 9783337266073

Printed in Europe, USA, Canada, Australia, Japan

Cover: Foto ©Thomas Meinert / pixelio.de

More available books at **www.hansebooks.com**

DOXOLOGIES, RESPONSES, &c.

No. 1. Old Hundred.

Isaac Watts, 1719.

Louis Bourgeois.

1. Praise God, from whom all blessings flow; Praise Him, all creatures here be-low;
2. E - ter - nal are Thy mer - cies, Lord! E - ter - nal truth at - tends Thy word;

Praise Him a - bove, ye heavenly host; Praise Father, Son, and Ho - ly Ghost.
Thy praise shall sound from shore to shore, Till suns shall rise and set no more. A - men.

2. Hursley.

Armstrong.

Peter Ritter.

"Do Thou Thy be - ne - dic - tion give On all who teach, on all who learn,

That all the Church may ho - lier live, And ev - ery lamp more brightly burn." A - men.

3. DOXOLOGY.

1 In every clime, by every tongue.
Be God's surpassing glory sung;
Let all the listening earth be taught
The wonders by our Saviour wrought.

2 Unfailing Comfort, Heavenly Guide,
Still in our longing hearts abide;
Still let mankind Thy blessings prove,
Spirit of mercy, truth, and love.

Rev. R. W. Kyle, 1775.

3

4. Gloria Patri.

Glory be to the }
Father, and } to the Son, and to the Ho-ly Ghost; the beginning,
As it was in }
is now, and } ev-er shall be, world without end. A-men.

5. The Lord's Prayer.

GREGORIAN.

1. Our Father who art in heaven,..................| Hal-lowed | be   thy |name. ||

Thy kingdom come: Thy will be done in......| earth, ·· as it | is   in | heaven;

2. Give us this | day our— | daily | bread : ||
    And forgive us our debts, as | we for- | give our | debtors.
3. And lead us not into temptation, but de- | liver | us from | evil: ||
    For thine is the kingdom, and the power, and the glory, for | ever. | A- — | men.

6. Our Father in Heaven.

SARA J. HALE.

E. L. WHITE, 1832.

1. Our Fa-ther in heaven, We hal-low Thy name! May Thy kingdom ho - ly, Ou
2. For-give our transgressions, And teach us to know That hum-ble compassion That

Our Father in Heaven.—Concluded.

earth be the same, O give to us dai - ly Our por - tion of bread,
par - dons each foe; Keep us from temp-ta - tion, From weakness and sin,

It is from Thy boun - ty That all must be fed.
And Thine be the glo - ry For ev - er— A - men.

7.   **Response after the Commandments.**

E. PAXTON HOOD.

IRA D. SANKEY, by per.

O Saviour and Master, these sayings of Thine, Help me to make them do-ings of mine.

REFRAIN.

Doings of mine, do-ings of mine, Oh help me to make them do-ings of mine.

5

8. Welcome, Hour of Praise and Prayer.

(SICILY.)

Sicilian Melody.

1. { Welcome, hour of sol-emn meet-ing, Welcome, hour of praise and prayer!
Far from earth - ly scenes re - treat-ing, In thy bless-ings we would share. }

Sa - cred sea - son, sa - cred sea - son, In Thy blessings we would share. A - men.

2 Be Thou near us, blessed Saviour,
  Still at morn and eve the same ;
Give us faith that cannot waver,
  Kindle in us heaven's own flame.
    Blessed Saviour,
  Kindle in us heaven's own flame.

3 When the fervent prayer is glowing,
  Sacred Spirit, hear that prayer ;
When the joyous song is flowing,
  Let that song Thine impress bear.
    Sacred Spirit,
  Let that song Thine impress bear.

9. THE CHILDREN'S SONG.

1 ONCE was heard the song of children,
  By the Saviour, when on earth ;
Joyful, in the sacred temple,
  Shouts of youthful praise had birth,
    And hosannas
  Loud to David's Son broke forth.

2 God o'er all, in heaven reigning !
  We this day Thy glory sing ;
Not with palms Thy pathway strewing,
  We would loftier tribute bring,—
    Glad hosannas
  To our Prophet, Priest and King.

English. Anon, 1848.

10. List to the Sabbath Bell.

(SPANISH HYMN.)

1. { Far, far o'er hill and dell, On the winds steal-ing }
   { List to the Sab-bath bell Sol-emn-ly peal-ing; } Hark, hark it seems to say,

2. { Far, far o'er hill and dell, On the winds steal-ing }
   { List to the Sab-bath bell Sol-emn-ly peal-ing; } Hark, hark it seems to say,

6

List to the Sabbath Bell.—Concluded.

Bid earthly cares a - way, Hal - low the Sabbath day, Fer - vent in feel - ing.
Turn from sin's joys a - way, To those which ne'er de-cay Heav - en re - veal - ing.

11. Christmas Carol.

D. M. MULOCH.

Old English.

1. God rest ye, lit - tle chil - dren, let nothing ye af-fright, For Je-sus Christ your
2. God rest ye, all good christians: up - on this bless-ed morn, The Lord of all good

Sav - iour was born on Christmas night, A - long the hills of Gal - i - lee the
Christians was of a wo-man born; Now all your sorrows He doth heal, your

white flocks sleeping lay, When Christ the child of Nazareth was born on Christmas Day.
sins He takes a - way, For Je-sus Christ your Saviour, was born on Christmas Day. A-men.

7

12.

Rejoice and be glad.

Rev. HORATIUS BONAR, 1874.

JOHN J. HUSBAND, 1796.

1. Re-joice and be glad! The Redeemer has come! Go look on His cra-dle, His cross, and His tomb.
2. Re-joice and be glad! It is sun-shine at last! The clouds have departed, the shadows are past.
3. Rejoice and be glad! For the blood hath been shed; Redemption is finished, the price hath been paid.
4. Re-joice and be glad! Now the pardon is free! The Just for the un-just has died on the tree.
5. Re-joice and be glad! For the Lamb that was slain O'er death is triumphant, and liveth a-gain.
6. Re-joice and be glad! For our King is on high, He pleadeth for us on His throne in the sky.
7. Re-joice and be glad! For He com-eth a - gain; He com-eth in glo-ry, the Lamb that was slain.

CHORUS. |1st. |2d.

Sound His praises, tell the Sto - ry,   Of Him who was slain; }
Sound His praises, tell with gladness, (Omit................... } He liv-eth a - gain.

For 7th Verse—He cometh a - gain. A - men.

13.   WE PRAISE THEE.

1 WE praise Thee, O God! for the Son of Thy love,
For Jesus who died and is now gone above.
CHORUS.
Hallelujah! Thine the glory, Hallelujah! Amen.
Hallelujah! Thine the glory, Revive us again.

2 We praise Thee, O God! for Thy Spirit of light,
Who has shown us our Saviour, and scattered our
night.—Cho.

3 All glory and praise to the Lamb that was slain,
Who has borne all our sins and has cleansed every
stain.—Cho.

14.   By cool Siloam's shady Rill.

R. HEBER. D. D.   (SILOAM.)   I. B. WOODBURY.

1. By cool Si - lo - am's shad - y rill How fair the lil - y grows! How sweet the breath be-
2. Lo! such the child whose ear-ly feet The paths of peace have trod; Whose secret heart, with in-
3. By cool Si - lo - am's shad - y rill The lil - y must de-cay; The rose that blooms be -

neath the hill, Of Sharon's dewy rose.
flu-ence sweet, Is upward drawn to God.
neath the hill Must shortly fade away. Amen.

4 O Thou, whose infant feet were found
    Within Thy Father's shrine,
Whose years, with changeless virtue crowned,
    Were all alike divine.

5 Dependent on Thy bounteous breath,
    We seek Thy grace alone
In childhood, manhood, age and death,
    To keep us still Thine own.

15.   Majestic Sweetness sits Enthroned.

S. STENNETT.   (ORTONVILLE.)   THOS. HASTINGS, Mus. Doc.

1. Ma - jes-tic sweetness sits enthroned Up-on the Saviour's brow; His head with radiant
2. No mor-tal can with Him compare, Among the sons of men; Fair-er is He than
3. He saw me plung'd in deep distress, He flew to my re - lief; For me He bore the

glories crown'd, His lips with grace o'er-flow, His lips with grace o'er-flow.
all the fair That fill the heavenly train, That fill the heavenly train.
shameful cross, And car-ried all my grief, And car-ried all my grief. A - men.

4 To Him I owe my life and breath,
   And all the joys I have;
He makes me triumph over death,
   He saves me from the grave.

5 To heaven, the place of His abode,
   He brings my weary feet;
Shows me the glories of my God,
   And makes my joy complete.

6 Since from His bounty I receive
   Such proofs of love divine,
Had I a thousand hearts to give,
   Lord! they should all be Thine.

16.   THINK GENTLY OF THE ERRING.

1 Think gently of the erring one!
   And let us not forget,
However darkly stained by sin,
   He is our brother yet.

2 Heir of the same inheritance,
   Child of the self-same God;
He hath but stumbled in the path,
   We have in weakness trod.

3 Forget not thou hast often sinned,
   And sinful yet must be:
Deal gently with the erring one,
   As God has dealt with thee.

17.   GOD'S LOVE TO US.
Tune.—SILOAM.

1 My God, how wonderful Thou art!
   Thy majesty how bright!
How glorious is Thy mercy-seat,
   In depths of burning light!

2 Yet I may love Thee too, O Lord,
   Almighty as Thou art;
For Thou hast stooped to ask of me
   The love of my poor heart.

3 No earthly father loves like Thee,
   No mother half so mild
Bears and forbears, as Thou hast done
   With me, Thy sinful child.

4 My God, how wonderful Thou art,
   Thou everlasting Friend!
On Thee I stay my trusting heart,
   Till faith in vision end.

F. W. Faber

18. Oh, Sing of His Mighty Love.

Rev. FRANK BOTTOME, D.D., 1869.

WM. B. BRADBURY, by per.

1. { Oh, bliss of the pu - ri-fied, bliss of the free, I plunge in the crimson tide open'd for me; }
   { O'er sin and un-clean-ness ex-ult - ing I stand; And point to the print of the nails in His hand. }

2. { Oh, bliss of the pu - ri-fied, Je - sus is mine, No longer in dread con-dem-na-tion I pine; }
   { In conscious sal-vation I sing of His grace, Who lifteth up-on me the light of His face. }

CHORUS.

Rit.

Oh, sing of His mighty love, Sing of His mighty love, Sing of His mighty love, Mighty to save.

Copyrighted, 1867, in Fresh Laurels.

3 O Jesus the crucified! Thee will I sing,
 My blessed Redeemer, my God and my King;
 My soul, filled with rapture, shall shout o'er the grave,
 And triumph in death in the "Mighty to Save."—CHO.

19. Day is Dying in the West.

MARY A. LATHBURY.

(EVENING PRAISE.)

WM. F. SHERWIN, by per.

1. Day is dying in the west; Heav'n is touching earth with rest; Wait and worship while the night
2. Lord of life, beneath the dome Of the U - ni-verse, Thy home, Gather us who seek Thy face

CHORUS.

Sets her evening lamps alight Thro' all the sky.   Holy, holy, ho-ly, Lord God of Hosts!
To the fold of Thy embrace, For Thou art high.

Day is Dying in the West.—Concluded.

Heav'n and earth are full of thee! Heav'n and earth are praising thee, O Lord most high! Amen.

20. O Day of Rest and Gladness.

C. WORDSWORTH. (MENDEBAS.) German Melody, arr. by LOWELL MASON.

1. { O day of rest and gladness, O day of joy and light, }
{ O balm of care and sad-ness, Most beautiful, most bright; } On thee, the high and lowly,

Bending before the throne, Sing Ho - ly, Ho-ly, Ho-ly, To the Great Three in One. Amen.

From "Spiritual Songs," by per. of the Century Company.

2 To-day on weary nations
The heavenly manna falls;
To holy convocations
The silver trumpet calls,
Where gospel light is glowing
With pure and radiant beams,
And living water flowing
With soul-refreshing streams.

3 New graces ever gaining
From this our day of rest,
We reach the rest remaining
To spirits of the blest.
To Holy Ghost be praises,
To Father and to Son;
The Church her voice upraises
To Thee, blest Three in One.

21. "IN EXCELSIS."

To EVENING PRAISE, page 10.

1 GLORY be to God on high,—
God, whose glory fills the sky;—
Peace on earth to man forgiven,—
Man, the well-beloved of heaven.
For God is nigh.—CHO.

2 Hail, by all Thy works adored!
Hail, the everlasting Lord!
Thee with thankful hearts we prove,—
God of power, and God of love!
For Thou art nigh.—CHO.

3 Jesus! in Thy name we pray,
Take, oh, take our sins away!
Powerful Advocate with God!
Justify us by Thy blood.
And be thou nigh.—CHO.
C. Wesley.

11

22. Anniversary Song.

E. L. WHITE, 1882.

1. Come, children, and join in our festival song, And hail the sweet joys which this day brings along;
2. Our Father, in heaven, we lift up to Thee Our voice of thanksgiving, our glad jubilee;
3. And if, ere this glad year has drawn to a close, Some lov'd one among us in death shall repose,

We'll join our glad voices in one song of praise, To God, who has kept us, and lengthen'd our days.
Oh, bless us and guide us, dear Saviour, we pray, That from Thy blest precepts we never may stray.
Grant, Lord, that the Spirit in heaven may dwell, In the bo-som of Jesus, where all shall be well.

REFRAIN.

Hal-le-lu-jah to the Lamb, Hallelujah to the Lamb, Hallelujah, hallelu-jah, hallelu-jah! A-men.

Hal-le - lu-jah, to the Lamb!

Instead of the REFRAIN *this* CHORUS *may be used when appropriate.*

CHORUS.

Happy greeting to all! Happy greeting to all! Happy greeting, happy greeting, happy greeting to all

Happy greeting, to all! Happy greeting, &c.

23. Sweet Home.

Rev. David Denham, 1826.

Sir Henry Rowley Bishop, 1823.

1. 'Mid scenes of confusion and creature complaints, How sweet to my soul is communion with saints;
2. Sweet bonds that unite all the children of peace! And thrice precious Jesus, whose love cannot cease

To find at the banquet of mercy there's room, And feel in the presence of Je - sus at
Tho' oft from Thy presence in sadness I roam, I long to be-hold Thee in glo - ry at

home, Home, home, sweet, sweet home, Prepare me, dear Sav-iour, for glo - ry, my home.
home, Home, home, sweet, sweet home, I long to be - hold Thee, in glo - ry at home.

3 While here in the valley of conflict I stay,
O give me submission and strength as my day;
In all my affliction to Thee would I come,
Rejoicing in hope of my glorious home.

4 Whate'er Thou deniest, O give me Thy grace,
The Spirit's sure witness,—the smiles of Thy
    face:
Endue me with patience to wait at Thy throne,
And find, even now, a sweet foretaste of home.

24. Tune—Anniversary Song, page 12.

1 I once was a stranger to grace and to God;
I knew not my danger, and felt not my load;
Though friends spoke in rapture of Christ
    on the tree,
Jehovah, my Saviour, seemed nothing to me.
[Omit Refrain.]

2 When free grace awoke me by light from on
    high,
Then legal fears shook me: I trembled to die:
No refuge, no safety, in self could I see:
Jehovah, Thou only my Saviour must be!

3 My terrors all vanished before His sweet name;
My guilty fears banished, with boldness I came
To drink at the fountain, life-giving and free:
Jehovah, my Saviour, is all things to me.

4 Jehovah, my Saviour, my treasure and boast!
Jehovah, my Saviour! I ne'er can be lost;
In Thee I shall conquer, by flood and by field,
Jehovah my Anchor, Jehovah my Shield!
Rev. R. M. McCheyne

25. Lord, dismiss us with Thy blessing.

Rev. JOHN FAWCETT.   (GREENVILLE.)   J. J. ROUSSEAU.

1. Lord, dis - miss us with Thy bless-ing; Fill our hearts with joy and peace:
2. Thanks we give, and ad - o - ra - tion, For Thy gos - pel's joy - ful sound;
3. Then, whene'er the sig - nal's giv - en Us from earth to call a - way,

Use repeat for hymns 26 and 27.

Let us each, Thy love pos - sess - ing, Tri - umph in re - deeming grace;
May the fruits of Thy sal - va - tion In our hearts and lives a - bound;
Borne on an - gels' wings to heav - en, Glad the summons to o - bey,

Oh, re - fresh us, Oh, re - fresh us Traveling thro' this wil - der - ness.
May Thy pres - ence, May Thy pres - ence With us ev - er - more be found.
May we ev - er, May we ev - er Reign with Christ in end - less day!

26.   THE LORD OUR GUIDE.

1 Gently, Lord, oh, gently lead us
  Through this lonely vale of tears;
Through the changes thou'st decreed us,
  Till our last great change appears.
When temptation's darts assail us,
  When in devious paths we stray,
Let Thy goodness never fail us,
  Lead us in Thy perfect way.

2 In the hour of pain and anguish,
  In the hour when death draws near,
Suffer not our hearts to languish,—
  Suffer not our souls to fear,
And when mortal life is ended,
  Bid us on Thy bosom rest,
Till, by angel-bands attended,
  We awake among the blest.

Thomas Hastings, Mus. Doc.

27.   AN OPENING PRAYER.

1 Heavenly Father, send Thy blessing
  On Thy children gathered here,.
May they all Thy name confessing,
  Be to Thee forever dear.
May they evermore be loving,
  Patient, dutiful, and pure,
And in trial steadfast proving,
  May their faith to death endure.

2 Holy Saviour, who in meekness
  Didst vouchsafe a child to be,
Guide their steps and help their weakness,
  Bless and make them like to Thee;
Bear Thy lambs when they are weary
  In Thine arms and on Thy breast,
Through life's desert dry and dreary,
  Bring them to Thy heavenly rest.

Christopher Wordsworth, D.D

28.   Guide me, O Thou Great Jehovah.

Rev. WM. WILLIAMS, 1778.   (SEGUR.)   J. P. HOLBROOK, by per.

```
1. Guide me, O, Thou great Je - ho-vah,  Pil-grim thro' this bar-ren land;   I am
2. O - pen now  the crys-tal fountain,   Whence the healing streams do flow;  Let the
3. When I  tread the verge of Jor-dan,  Bid my  anx-ious fears sub-side;   Death of
```

```
weak, but Thou art might-y;    Hold me  with   Thy pow'r-ful hand;   Bread of
fie - ry, cloudy  pil - lar     Lead me  all    my jour - ney through;  Strong de -
death, and hell's destruc-tion  Land me  safe   on Ca - naan's side;   Songs of
```

```
heav - en,   Bread of heav - en,   Feed me   till   I want  no   more.
liv - erer,  Strong de - liv - erer,  Be  Thou  still   my strength and  shield.
prais - es,  Songs of  prais - es,  I   will   ev - er give  to   Thee.
```

29.   A PRAYER FOR GOD'S PRESENCE.
Tune—GREENVILLE.

1 SAVIOUR! visit Thy plantation;
   Grant us, Lord! a gracious rain;
   All will come to desolation
     Unless Thou return again.
      Lord! revive us,
   All our help must come from Thee.

2 Break the tempter's fatal power;
   Turn the stony heart to flesh;
   And begin from this good hour
     To revive Thy work afresh.
      Lord! revive us,
   All our help must come from Thee.
Rev. John Newton.

30.   Hymns of Grateful Love.

JAMES J. CUMMINS.   WM. B. BRADBURY, by per.

1. Shall hymns of grateful love Thro' heav'n's high arches ring, And all the hosts a -
2. Shall ev - ery ransomed tribe Of Adam's scattered race, To Christ all powers as -
3. Shall they a - dore the Lord Who bought them with His blood, And all the love re -

FULL CHORUS. *ff*

bove Their songs of tri - umph sing? And shall not we take up the strain, And
cribe, Who saved them by His grace?
cord That led them home to God?

ff   *pp* Echo at a distance.

send the ech - o back a - gain? And send the ech - o, *send the ech - o,*

ff   *pp*   *ff*

Send the ech-o, *send the ech-o,* Send the ech - o, send the ech - o back a - gain?

31. Beulah Land.

Rev. Edgar Page Stites.   Jno. R. Sweney, by per.

1. I've reach'd the land of corn and wine, And all its rich-es free-ly mine; Here
2. The Saviour comes and walks with me, And sweet com-munion here have we; He
3. A sweet perfume up - on the breeze Is borne from ev - er ver - nal trees, And
4. The zephyrs seem to float to me, Sweet sounds of heaven's mel - o - dy, As

shines undimm'd, one blissful day, For all my night has pass'd a-way. O Beulah land, sweet
gent - ly leads me with His hand, For this is heaven's border-land.
flow'rs that nev-er fad - ing grow Where streams of life forev-er flow.
angels, with the white-robed throng, Join in the sweet redemption-song.

Chorus.

Beulah land, As on thy highest mount I stand, I look a-way a - cross the sea, Where

mansions are prepared for me, And view the shining glory shore, My heav'n, my home forevermore.

17

82. Oh! worship the King.

ROBERT GRANT, 1880.   (LYONS.)   F. J. HAYDN, 1770.

1. Oh! wor-ship the King, all - glo-rious a - bove, Oh! grate-ful - ly
2. Oh! tell of His might, oh! sing of His grace, Whose robe is the
3. Thy boun - ti - ful care what tongue can re - cite! It breathes in the
4. Frail child-ren of dust, and fee - ble as frail, In Thee do we

sing His pow - er and love, Our Shield and De - fen - der, the An - cient of
light, whose can - o - py space; His chariots of wrath the deep thun-der-clouds
air, it shines in the light; It streams from the hills, it descends to the
trust, nor find Thee to fail; Thy mer-cies how ten - der, how firm to the

days, Pa - vil - ioned in splen-dor, and gird - ed with praise,
form, And dark is His path on the wings of the storm.
plain, And sweet - ly dis - tills in the dew and the rain.
end, Our Ma - ker, De - fen - der, Re - deem - er, and Friend. A - men.

83.   JESUS OUR KING.

1 Ye servants of God! your Master proclaim,
And publish abroad His wonderful name ;
The name, all-victorious, of Jesus extol ;
His kingdom is glorious, and rules over all.

2 God ruleth on high, almighty to save ;
And still He is nigh—His presence we have :
The great congregation His triumph shall sing,
Ascribing salvation to Jesus, our King.

3 Then let us adore, and give Him His right,
All glory and power, and wisdom and might,
All honor and blessing, with angels above,
And thanks never ceasing, and infinite love.

Charles Wesley, 1744, ab.

84.   EASTER.

1 Smile praises, O sky! soft breathe them, O air !
Below and on high, and everywhere ;
The black troop of storms has scatter'd and fled,
The Lord hath arisen, unharm'd from the dead.

2 Sweep tides of rich music, the new world along,
And pour in full measure, sweet lyres, your song,
Sing, sing, for He liveth, He lives, as He said :
The Lord hath arisen unharmed from the dead.

3 Clap, clap your hands, mountains; ye valleys,
resound ;   [sound :
Leap, leap for joy, fountains, ye hills, catch the
All triumph! He liveth, He lives, as He said ;
The Lord hath arisen unharmed from the dead.

35. Prayer for Guidance.

JAMES EDMESTON.   J. DOWLAND, arr. by ALICE PELOUBET NORTON.

1. Lead us, heav'nly Fa - ther, lead us, O'er the world's tem - pest - uous sea;
2. Sav - iour, breathe for-give - ness o'er us; All our weak - ness Thou dost know;
3. Spir - it of our God de - scending, Fill our hearts with heaven - ly joy;

Guard us, guide us, keep us, feed us, For we have no help but Thee;
Thou didst tread this earth be - fore us, Thou didst feel its keen - est woe;
Love, with ev - ery pas - sion blend-ing, Pleas-ure that can nev - er cloy;

Yet pos-sess-ing, Ev - ery blessing, If our God our Fa - ther be:
Lone and drea - ry, Faint and wea - ry, Thro' the des - ert Thou didst go:
Thus pro - vid - ed, Pardon'd, guid-ed, Noth - ing can our peace de - stroy:

Lead us, heav'n-ly Fa - ther, lead us, For we have no help but Thee.
Sav - iour, breathe for-give - ness o'er us, All our weak-ness Thou dost know.
Spir - it of our God, de-scend - ing, Fill our hearts with heavenly joy. A - men.

86. Sweet By-and-By.

S. FILLMORE BENNETT.   JOS. P. WEBSTER, by per. arr.

1. There's a land that is fair - er than day, And by faith we can see it a - far;
2. We shall sing on that beau-ti - ful shore The mel - o - di - ous songs of the blest,
3. To our boun-ti - ful Fa-ther a - bove, We will of - fer our trib-ute of praise,

For the Fa-ther waits o - ver the way, To pre-pare us a dwelling place there.
And our spir-its shall sor-row no more, Not a sigh for the blessing of rest.
For the glo - ri - ous gift of His love, And the blessings that hal-low our days.

CHORUS.

In the sweet   by and by,   We shall meet on that beautiful shore,

In the sweet   by-and-by,   by - and-by,

In the sweet   by - and - by,   We shall meet on that beauti-ful shore.

by-and-by, In the sweet by-and-by,

Whiter than Snow.

JAMES NICHOLSON.   WM. G. FISCHER, by per.

1. Dear Je - sus, I long to be per - fect - ly whole; I want Thee for -
2. Dear Je - sus, come down from Thy throne in the skies, And help me to
3. Dear Je - sus, for this, I most hum - bly en - treat; I wait, bless - ed

ev - er to live in my soul; Break down ev - ery i - dol, cast out ev - ery foe;
make a com-plete sac - ri - fice; I give up my - self, and what - ev - er I know—
Lord, sitting low at Thy feet, By faith, for my cleansing, I see the blood flow—

CHORUS.

Now wash me, and I shall be whit - er than snow. Whit - er than snow, yes,
Now wash me, and I shall be whit - er than snow.
Now wash me, and I shall be whit - er than snow.

whit - er than snow; Now wash me, and I shall be whit - er than snow.

88. Christt for the World we sing.

Rev. S. Wolcott, D.D.   (CUTTING.)   Wm. F. Sherwin, by per.

1. Christ for the world we sing; The world to Christ we bring, With lov-ing zeal; The poor, and
2. Christ for the world we sing; The world to Christ we bring, With fervent pray'r; The wayward
3. Christ for the world we sing; The world to Christ we bring, With one ac-cord; With us the
4. Christ for the world we sing; The world to Christ we bring, With joy-ful song; The new-born

them that mourn, The faint and over-borne, Sin-sick and sorrow-worn, Whom Christ doth heal.
and the lost, By restless passions tossed, Redeemed at countless cost, From dark despair.
work to share, With us reproach to dare, With us the cross to bear, For Christ our Lord.
souls, whose days, Reclaim'd from error's ways, Inspir'd with hope and praise, To Christ belong. *Amen.*

89. My faith Looks up to Thee.

Dr. Ray Palmer.   (OLIVET.)   Lowell Mason.

1. My faith looks up to Thee, Thou Lamb of Cal-va-ry, Saviour di-vine! Now hear me
2. May Thy rich grace impart Strength to my fainting heart; My zeal in-spire; As Thou hast

while I pray, Take all my guilt a-way, Oh, let me from this day Be whol-ly Thine!
died for me, Oh, may my love to Thee Pure, warm, and changless be, A liv-ing fire.

My faith Looks up to Thee.—Concluded.

3 While life's dark maze I tread,
And griefs around me spread;
Be Thou my guide;
Bid darkness turn to day;
Wipe sorrow's tears away;
Nor let me ever stray
From Thee aside.

4 When ends life's transient dream;
When death's cold, sullen stream
Shall o'er me roll;
Blest Saviour, then, in love,
Fear and distrust remove;
O bear me safe above,—
A ransomed soul.

40.   Come, Thou Almighty King.

C. WESLEY.   (ITALIAN HYMN.)   F. GIARDINI.

1. Come, Thou al-mighty King, Help us Thy name to sing, Help us to praise: Fa-ther! all
2. Come, Thou in-carnate Word, Gird on Thy mighty sword; Our prayer attend; Come, and Thy

glo - ri-ous, O'er all vic - to - ri-ous, Come, and reign o - ver us, Ancient of Days!
peo - ple bless, And give Thy word success—Spir-it of ho - li-ness! On us de-scend.

3 Come, holy Comforter!
Thy sacred witness bear,
In this glad hour:
Thou, who almighty art,
Now rule in every heart,
And ne'er from us depart,
Spirit of power!

4 To the great One in Three,
The highest praises be,
Hence evermore!
His sovereign majesty
May we in glory see,
And to eternity
Love and adore.

41.   LOYALTY.

1 SAVIOUR, who died for me,
Thy love, so full, so free,
Claims all my powers.
Be this my purpose high,
To serve Thee till I die,
Whether my path shall lie
'Mid thorns or flowers.

2 May it be joy to me
To follow only Thee,—
Thine to the end.
For Thee, I'll do and dare,
For Thee, the cross I'll bear,
To Thee, direct my prayer,
On Thee depend.

Mary Mason. alt.

23

42. Glorious Things of Thee are Spoken.

Rev. JOHN NEWTON, 1779.　　　　　(AUTUMN.)　　　　　Spanish, from MAREOHIO.

1. Glo - rious things of Thee are spok - en, Zi - on, cit - y of our God!...
2. See, the streams of liv - ing wa - ters, Springing from e - ter - nal love,...
3. Round each hab - i - ta - tion hov - ering, See the cloud and fire ap - pear!...

He, whose word can not be bro - ken, Formed thee for His own a - bode ;
Well sup - ply Thy sous and daughters, And all fear of want re - move :
For a glo - ry and a cover - ing, Showing that the Lord is near;

On the Rock of A - ges found - ed, What can shake Thy sure re - pose?
Who can faint, while such a riv - er Ev - er flows their thirst t' as-suage?
He who gives them dai - ly man - na, He who list - ens when they cry, —

With sal - va - tion's walls sur-round - ed, Thou mayst smile at all Thy foes.
Grace, which, like the Lord, the giv - er, Nev - er fails from age to age.
Let Him hear the loud ho - san - na, Ris - ing to His throne on high.

43. Praise to Thee, Thou great Creator.

Rev. John Fawcett, 1767.   (TALMAR.)   I. B. Woodbury.

1. Praise to Thee, Thou great Cre - a - tor! Praise be
2. Fa - ther, Source of all com - pas - sion, Pure un -
3. For ten thou - sand bless - ings giv - en, For the
4. Joy - ful - ly on earth a - dore Him, Till in

Thine from ev - ery tongue; Join, my soul, with ev - ery
bound - ed grace is Thine; Hail the God of our sal -
rich - est gifts be - stowed, Sound His praise through earth and
Heaven our song we raise; There, en - rap - tured fall be -

crea - ture, Join the u - ni - ver - sal song.
va - tion, Praise Him for His love di - - vine.
heav - en, Sound Je - ho - vah's praise a - - loud.
fore Him, Lost in won - der, love, and praise. A - men.

44. COMING TO OUR FATHER.

1 Take me, O my Father! take me,
   Take me, save me, through Thy Son;
   That, which Thou wouldst have me, make me,
   Let Thy will in me be done.

2 Long from Thee my footsteps straying,
   Thorny proved the way I trod;
   Weary come I now, and praying—
   Take me to Thy love, my God!

3 Fruitless years with grief recalling,
   Humbly I confess my sin;

At Thy feet, O Father! falling,
   To Thy household take me in.

4 Freely now to Thee I proffer
   This relenting heart of mine;
   Freely, life and soul I offer—
   Gift unworthy love like Thine.

5 Father! take me; all forgiving,
   Fold me to Thy loving breast;
   In Thy love for ever living,
   I must be for ever blessed!

Ray Palmer. 1864.

45. Yield Not to Temptation.

H. R. PALMER.   H. R. PALMER, by per.

1. Yield not to tempta . tion, For yielding is sin, Each vic-t'ry will help you
2. Shun e - vil com-pan-ions, Bad language dis - dain, God's name hold in reverence,
3. To him that o'er-com-eth God giv - eth a crown, Thro' faith we shall con-quer,

Some oth - er to win; Fight man-ful - ly onward, Dark passions sub - due,
Nor take it in vain; Be thoughtful and earnest, Kind-heart-ed and true,
Though oft-en cast down; He who is our Saviour, Our strength will re - new.

CHORUS.

Look ev - er to Je - sus, He'll car - ry you through. Ask the Saviour to help you,
Look ev - er to Je - sus, He ll car - ry you through,
Look ev - er to Je - sus, He'll car - ry you through.

Comfort, strengthen, and keep you; He is willing to aid you, He will carry you through.

28

46. ## When, His Salvation Bringing.

Rev. JOHN KING.   W. A. MOZART.

1. When, His sal-va-tion bringing, To Zi-on, Je-sus came, The children all stood
2. And since the Lord re-tain-eth His love for children still— Tho' now as King He
3. For, should we fail pro-claim-ing Our great Re-deemer's praise, The stones, our silence

sing-ing, "Ho-san-na to His name!" Nor did their zeal of-fend Him, But
reign-eth On Zi-on's heaven-ly hill— We'll flock a-round His ban-ner Who
sham-ing, Might well "Ho-san-na!" raise. But shall we ou-ly ren-der The

as He rode a-long He let them still attend Him. And smiled to hear their song.
sits up-on the throne, And cry aloud, "Hosan-na To David's roy-al Son!"
tribute of our words? No! While our hearts are tender They too shall be the Lord's. A-men.

47.   JESUS OUR LEADER.

1 O WHEN shall I see Jesus,
   And reign with Him above;
   And from that flowing fountain,
   Drink everlasting love?
   When shall I be delivered
   From this vain world of sin,
   And with my blessed Jesus,
   Drink endless pleasures in?

2 But now I am a soldier,
   My Captain's gone before;
   He's given me my orders,
   And bid me not give o'er;
   And since He has proved faithful,
   A righteous crown He'll give,
   And all His valiant soldiers
   Eternal life shall have.

3 Whene'er you meet with troubles
   And trials on your way,
   O! cast your care on Jesus,
   And don't forget to pray.
   Gird on the heavenly armor
   Of faith, and hope, and love;
   Then, when the combat's ended,
   He'll carry you above.
                                   Rev. JOHN LELAND.

48.   THE SECOND COMING.

1 WHEN shall the voice of singing
   Flow joyfully along,
   When hill and valley, ringing
   With one triumphant song,
   Proclaim the contest ended,
   And Him who once was slain
   A second time descended
   In righteousness to reign?
                                   JAMES EDMESTON.

49. I need Thee every Hour.

Mrs. ANNIE S. HAWKS.

Rev. ROBERT LOWRY, by per.

1. I need Thee every hour, Most gracious Lord; No tender voice like Thine Can peace af-ford.
2. I need Thee every hour, Stay Thou near by; Temptations lose their pow'r When Thou art nigh.
3. I need Thee every hour, Teach me Thy will; And Thy rich promis-es In me ful-fill.
4. I need Thee every hour, Most Ho-ly One; Oh, make me Thine indeed, Thou bless-ed Son.

REFRAIN.

I need Thee; oh! I need Thee; Every hour I need Thee; O bless me now, my Saviour! I come to Thee.

Copyright, 1872, by Robert Lowry.

50. May the grace of Christ.

J. NEWTON.

(SICILY.)

Sicilian Melody.

1. May the grace of Christ our Saviour, And the Father's boundless love,
2. Thus may we a-bide in un-ion With each oth-er and the Lord;

With the Ho-ly Spir-it's fa-vor, Rest up-on us from a-bove!
And pos-sess in sweet com-munion, Joys which earth can-not af-ford. A-men.

28

51. Sweet the Moments.

WALTER SHIRLEY, 1771.

G. B. VIOTTI, arr. by H. P. MAIN.

1. Sweet the moments, rich in blessing, Which be-fore the cross I spend,
2. Tru - ly bless-ed is this sta-tion, Low be-fore His cross to lie;

Life, and health, and peace pos-sess-ing, From the sin - ner's dy - ing Friend.
While I see di - vine com - pas-sion Beam - ing in His gra - cious eye.

Love and grief my heart di - vid-ing, With my tears His feet I'll bathe;
Here I'll sit, for ev - er view-ing, Mer - cy streaming in His blood;

Con - stant still, in faith a - bid-ing, Life de - riv - ing from His death.
Pre - cious drops my soul be - dew-ing, Plead, and claim my peace with God.

---

52.   DOXOLOGY.

1 WORSHIP, honor, glory, blessing,
   Lord, we offer to Thy name:
Young and old their praise expressing,
   Join Thy goodness to proclaim.
As the saints in Heaven adore Thee,
   We would bow before Thy throne;
As the angels serve before Thee,
   So on earth Thy will be done!
Edward Osler, 1836.

53.   DOXOLOGY.

GLORY be to God the Father,
   Glory be to God the Son,
Glory be to God the Spirit,
   Great Jehovah, Three in One.
H. Bonar, D.D.

54. All to Christ I Owe.

Mrs. ELVINA M. HALL, 1865.　　　　　　　　　　　　JOHN T. GRAPE. by per.

1. I hear the Sav - iour say, Thy strength in - deed is small;
2. Lord, now in - deed I find Thy power, and Thine a - lone,

Child of weak - ness, watch and pray, Find in Me thine all in all.
Can change the lep - er's spots, And melt the heart of stone.

CHORUS.

Je - sus paid it all, All to Him I owe;

Sin had left a crim - son stain: He washed it white as snow.

3 For nothing good have I
　Whereby Thy grace to claim—
I'll wash my garment white
　In the blood of Calvary's Lamb.—CHO.

4 And when before the throne
　I stand in Him complete,
I'll lay my trophies down,
　All down at Jesus' feet.—CHO

55. Jesus, Thy name I Love.

J. G. DECK.　　　　　　(LYTE.)　　　　　J. P. HOLBROOK. by per.

1. Je - sus, Thy name I love, All oth - er names above, Je - sus, my Lord! Oh, Thou art
2. Thou blessed Son of God, Hast bought me with Thy blood, Je-sus, my Lord! Oh, how great
3. When un - to Thee I flee, Thou wilt my ref - uge be, Je - sus, my Lord! What need I
4. Soon Thou wilt come again! I shall be hap-py then, Je - sus, my Lord! Then Thine own

all to me! Nothing to please I see, Nothing a - part from Thee, Je - sus, my Lord!
is Thy love, All oth - er loves a-bove, Love that I dai - ly prove, Je - sus, my Lord!
now to fear? What earthly grief or care, Since Thou art ev - er near? Je - sus, my Lord!
face I'll see, Then I shall like Thee be, Then ev - er-more with Thee, Je - sus, my Lord!

56. Life's Battle-Field.

Unison.

1. Soldier on life's bat - tle-field Be thou valiant, bold, and strong; In the strife, with

CHORUS.

cheer-ful zeal, Urge the Saviour's cause a - long. Onward, onward, to glo - ry!

Yield not to the wi - ly foe; Vict'ry and heav'n are before thee, Shout your triumphs as you go.

2 Jesus calls us to the field,
　He will lead us evermore;
　'Neath His banner ne'er to yield,
　Till the mighty conflict's o'er.

3 Then, in yonder world of light,
　We will lay our armor down;
　And, 'mid throngs of angels bright,
　Each receive a starry crown.

57. I Love Thy Kingdom Lord.

TIMOTHY DWIGHT, D. D. 1800.　　　(SHIRLAND.)　　　S. STANLEY.

1. I love Thy king - dom, Lord,— The house of Thine a - bode,
2. I love Thy church, O God! Her walls be - fore Thee stand,

The church our blest Re - deem - er saved, With His own precious blood.
Dear as the ap - ple of Thine eye, And grav - en on Thy hand. A-men.

3 For her my tears shall fall,
  For her my prayers ascend,
  To her my cares and toils be given,
  Till toils and cares shall end.

4 Beyond my highest joy
  I prize her heavenly ways,
  Her sweet communion, solemn vows,
  Her hymns of love and praise.

5 Jesus, thou Friend divine,
  Our Saviour and our King,
  Thy hand from every snare and foe,
  Shall great deliverance bring.

6 Sure as Thy truth shall last,
  To Zion shall be given
  The brightest glories earth can yield
  And brighter bliss of heaven.

58. A CALL TO PRAYER.

1 Jesus, who knows full well
  The heart of every saint,
  Invites us all our grief to tell,
  To pray and never faint.

2 He bows His gracious ear,—
  We never plead in vain;
  Then let us wait till He appear,
  And pray, and pray again.

3 Jesus, the Lord, will hear
  His chosen when they cry;
  Yes, though He may a while forbear,
  He'll help them from on high.

4 Then let us earnest cry,
  And never faint in prayer;
  He sees, He hears, and, from on high,
  Will make our cause His care.

J. Newton.

59. Come, Kingdom of our God.

H. B. JOHNS.   (LUTHER.)   THOS. HASTINGS.

1, Come, kingdom of our God, Sweet reign of light and love! Shed peace and hope and
2. O - ver our spir - its first Ex - tend thy healing reign; There raise and quench the
3. Come, kingdom of our God! And make the broad earth thine; Stretch o'er her lands and
4. Soon may all tribes be blest With fruit from life's glad tree; And in its shade like

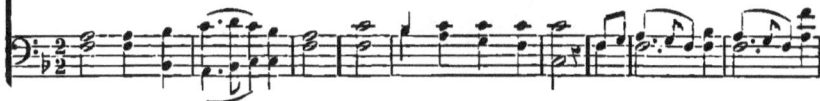

joy abroad, And wisdom from a - bove, And wis - dom from a - bove.
sa - cred thirst, That nev-er pains a - gain, That nev - er pains a - gain.
isles the rod That flowers with grace divine, That flowers with grace di - vine.
brothers rest, Sons of one fam - i - ly, Sons of one fam - i - ly. A-men.

---

60.   COME, LORD JESUS.

1 O Thou whom we adore!
    To bless our earth again,
  Assume Thine own almighty power,
    And o'er the nations reign.

2 The world's Desire and Hope,
    All power to Thee is given;
  Now set the last great empire up,
    Eternal Lord of heaven!

3 A gracious Saviour, Thou
    Wilt all Thy creatures bless;
  And every knee to Thee shall bow,
    And every tongue confess.

4 According to Thy word,
    Now be Thy grace revealed;
  And with the knowledge of the Lord,
    Let all the earth be filled.
                   Charles Wesley.

61.   SABBATH DAY.

1 This is the day of light;
    Let there be light to-day;
  O Day Spring, rise upon our night,
    And chase its gloom away.

2 This is the day of rest:
    Our failing strength renew;
  On weary brain and troubled breast
    Shed Thou Thy freshening dew.

3 This is the day of peace:
    Thy peace our spirits fill;
  Bid Thou the blasts of discord cease,
    The waves of strife be still.

4 This is the day of prayer:
    Let earth to heaven draw near:
  Lift up our hearts to seek Thee there;
    Come down to meet us here.
                   John Ellerton.

62.   Draw Me Nearer.

FANNY J. CROSBY.

W. H. DOANE, by per.

1. I am Thine, O Lord, I have heard Thy voice, And it told Thy love to me;
2. Con-se-crate me now to Thy ser-vice, Lord, By the pow'r of grace di-vine;
3. O the pure de-light of a sin gle hour That be-fore Thy throne I spend,
4. There are depths of love that I can-not know Till I cross the nar-row sea,

But I long to rise in the arms of faith, And be clos-er drawn to Thee.
Let my soul look up with a steadfast hope, And my will be lost in Thine.
When I kneel in pray'r, and with Thee my God, I commune as friend with friend.
There are heights of joy that I may not reach Till I rest in peace with Thee.

Draw me near - er, near-er, bless-ed Lord, To the cross where Thou hast died,

near-er, near-er,

Draw me near - er, near-er, near-er, blessed Lord, To Thy precious, bleeding side,

34

68. The Valley of Blessing.

Mrs. ANNIE WITTENMYER.　　　　　　　　　　　WM. G. FISCHER, by per.

1. I have en-ter'd the val-ley of blessing so sweet, And Je - sus a - bides with me there;
2. There is peace in the val-ley of blessing so sweet, And plen - ty the land doth im-part,
3. There is love in the val-ley of blessing so sweet, Such as none but the blood-wash'd may feel,
4. There's a song in the val-ley of blessing so sweet, That an - gels would fain join the strain,

And His spirit and blood make my cleansing complete, And His per-fect love cast-eth out fear.
And there's rest for the wea - ry-worn trav-el-er's feet, And joy for the sor-row-ing heart.
When heaven comes down redeemed spir - its to greet, And Christ sets His cov - e - nant seal.
As with rap-tur-ous praises we bow at His feet, Crying, "Worthy the Lamb that was slain."

CHORUS.

Oh, come to the val - ley of blessing so sweet, Where Je - sus will fullness be-stow--

And believe, and receive, and con-fess Him, That all His sal - va - tion may know.

35

64. Welcome, delightful Morn.

HAYWARD. (LISCHER.) FRED. SCHNEIDER, 1839.

1. Welcome de-light-ful morn, Thou day of sa-cred rest; I hail thy kind re-turn;—
2. Now may the King descend, And fill His throne of grace; Thy sceptre, Lord ex-tend,
3. Descend ce-les-tial Dove, With all thy quickening pow'rs; Disclose a Saviour's love,

Lord, make these moments blest; From the low train Of mor-tal toys, I soar to reach Im-
While saints address Thy face: Let sinners feel Thy quickening word, And learn to know And
And bless these sa-cred hours: Then shall my soul New life obtain, Nor Sabbaths be En-

mor-tal joys, I soar.... to reach Im-mor-tal joys.
fear the Lord. And learn.. to know And fear the Lord.
joyed in vain, Nor Sab-baths be En-joyed in vain. A-men.

I soar to reach Im-mor-tal joys.

65. PSALM 84.

1 LORD of the worlds above!
　How pleasant, and how fair,
　The dwellings of Thy love,
　Thine earthly temples are!
To Thine abode my heart aspires,
With warm desires to see my God.

2 Oh, happy souls who pray,
　Where God appoints to hear!
　Oh, happy men who pay

Their constant service there!
They praise Thee still; and happy they,
Who love the way to Zion's hill.

3 They go from strength to strength,
　Through this dark vale of tears,
　Till each arrives at length,
　Till each in heaven appears;
Oh, glorious seat, when God our King,
Shall hither bring our willing feet!

Isaac Watts.

66.   Arise, my Soul, Arise.

Rev. CHARLES WESLEY, 1742, (ab.).   (LENOX.)   LEWIS EDSON, 1781.

1. A - rise, my soul, a - rise; Shake off thy guilt-y fears; The bleeding Sac - ri -fice

In my be-half appears: Be - fore the throne my sure - ty stands, My

Before the throne my surety stands, My name is writ - ten

name is writ - ten on His hands, My name is writ-ten on His hands.   A-men.

on His hands, My name is writ - - ten on His hands.

2 The Father hears Him pray,
  His dear anointed one;
He cannot turn away
  The presence of His Son:
His spirit answers to the blood,
And tells me I am born of God.

3 My God is reconciled;
  His pardoning voice I hear;
He owns me for His child;
  I can no longer fear;
With confidence I now draw nigh,
And Father, Abba Father, cry.

67.   SALVATION.

1 BLOW ye the trumpet, blow,
  The gladly-solemn sound;
Let all the nations know,
  To earth's remotest bound,

The year of jubilee is come;
Return, ye ransomed sinners, home.

2 Exalt the lamb of God,
  The sin-atoning Lamb;
Redemption by His blood,
  Through all the lands proclaim.
    The year, &c.

3 The gospel trumpet hear,
  The news of pardoning grace;
Ye happy souls, draw near,
  Behold your Saviour's face.
    The year, &c.

4 Jesus, our great High Priest,
  Has full atonement made;
Ye weary spirits, rest;
  Ye mourning souls, be glad.
    The year, &c.

Charles Wesley, 1750.

68. More Love to Thee, O Christ.

Mrs. Elizabeth Prentiss. 1856.   W. H. Doane, by per.

1. More love to Thee, O Christ! More love to Thee; Hear Thou the pray'r I make On bended
2. Once earthly joy I craved Sought peace and rest; Now Thee a-lone I seek, Give what is
3. Let sor-row do its work, Send grief and pain; Sweet are Thy messengers, Sweet their re-
4. Then shall my lat-est breath, Whisper Thy praise, This be the parting cry My heart shall

knee; This is my earnest plea, More love, O Christ, to Thee, More love to Thee! More love to Thee!
best: This all my pray'r shall be,
frain, When they can sing with me, —
raise; This still its prayer shall be:

Copyright, 1870, in Songs of Devotion

69. Saviour, Source of every Blessing.

Robert Robinson, 1757, alt.   (BARTIMEUS.)   Stephen Jenks, 1800.

1. Sav-iour, source of ev-ery blessing, Tune my heart to grate-ful lays;
2. Teach me some me-lo-dious measure, Sung by rap-tured saints a-bove;
3. Thou didst seek me when a stranger, Wand-'ring from the fold of God;
4. By Thy hand re-stored, de-fend-ed, Safe through life, thus far, I'm come;

Streams of mer-cy, nev-er ceasing, Call for ceaseless songs of praise.
Fill my soul with sac-red pleasure, While I sing re-deem-ing love.
Thou, to save my soul from dan-ger, Didst re-deem me with Thy blood.
And, O Lord, when life is end-ed, Bring me to my heavenly home. A - men.

38

70.   Love Divine, all Love Excelling.

CHARLES WESLEY.   (EMERALD.)   Maj. WHITMORE.

1. Love divine, all love excelling,—Joy of heaven, to earth come down, Fix in us Thy humble dwelling, All Thy faithful mercies crown; Jesus! Thou art all compas-sion, Pure, unbounded love Thou art, Vis - it us with Thy sal-va-tion, En - ter ev - ery trembling heart.

2 Breathe, oh, breathe Thy loving Spirit
  Into every troubled breast !
Let us all in Thee inherit,
  Let us find Thy promised rest:
Come, almighty to deliver,
  Let us all Thy life receive !
Speedily return, and never,
  Never more Thy temples leave !

3 Finish, then, Thy new creation,
  Pure, unspotted may we be :
Let us see our whole salvation
  Perfectly secured by Thee !
Changed from glory into glory,
  Till in heaven we take our place;
Till we cast our crowns before Thee,
  Lost in wonder, love, and praise.

71.

1 SOUL, then know thy full salvation,
  Rise o'er sin, and fear, and care;
Joy, to find in every station
  Something still to do or bear.
Think what Spirit dwells within thee;
  Think what Father's smiles are thine;
Think that Jesus died to win thee !
  Child of heaven, canst thou repine?

2 Haste thee on from grace to glory,
  Armed by faith and winged by prayer !
Heaven's eternal day's before thee,
  God's own hand shall guide thee there:
Soon shall close thy earthly mission,
  Soon shall pass thy pilgrim days,
Hope shall change to glad fruition,
  Faith to sight, and prayer to praise.
          Rev. Henry F. Lyte.

72. Heaven is my Home.

T. R. TAYLOR. (OAK.) LOWELL MASON, by per.

1. I'm but a stranger here, Heav'n is my home;
   Earth is a desert drear, Heav'n is my home;
2. What tho' the tempest rage? Heav'n &c.
   Short is my pilgrimage, Heav'n is my home;

Danger and sorrow stand Round me on every hand,
And time's wild, wintry blast, Soon shall be overpast,

Heaven is my Fa - therland, Heaven is my home.
I shall reach home at last,— Heaven is my home. *Amen.*

3 Therefore I murmur not,—
  Heaven is my home;
Whate'er my earthly lot,
  Heaven is my home;
And I shall surely stand
There, at my Lord's right hand;
Heaven is my Fatherland,
  Heaven is my home.

Copyright used by per. of Oliver Ditson & Co

73. Saviour! teach me Day by Day.

JANE E. LEESON, 1842. (FULTON.) W. B. BRADBURY, by per.

1. Sav - iour! teach me, day by day, Love's sweet les - son to o - bey;
2. With a child - like heart of love, At Thy bid - ding may I move;
3. Teach me all Thy steps to trace, Strong to fol - low in Thy grace;
4. Thus may I re - joice to show That I feel the love I owe;

Sweeter les - son can - not be, Lov - ing Him who first loved me.
Prompt to serve and fol - low Thee, Lov - ing Him who first loved me.
Learning how to love from Thee, Lov - ing Him who first loved me.
Singing, till! Thy face I see, Of His love who first loved me. *A - men.*

40

74. Every Day and Hour.

FANNY J. CROSBY.   W. H. DOANE.

Slowly.

1. Sav-iour, more than life to me, I am clinging, clinging close to Thee;
   Let Thy pre-cious blood ap-plied, Keep me ev-er, ev-er near Thy side.

2. Thro' this changing world be-low, Lead me gen-tly, gen-tly as I go;
   Trust-ing Thee, I can-not stray, I can nev-er, nev-er lose my way.

3. Let me love Thee more and more, Till this fleet-ing, fleeting life is o'er;
   Till my soul is lost in love, In a brighter, brighter world a-bove.

REFRAIN.

Ev-ery-day, ev-ery-day, Let me feel Thy cleansing power;

and hour, and hour,

May Thy ten-der love to me Bind me clos-er, clos-er, Lord, to Thee.

Copyright, 1875, by Biglow & Main.

75.

Tune.—SAVIOUR! TEACH ME,

1 BROTHER,* though from yonder sky
Cometh neither voice nor cry,
Yet we know for thee to-day,
Every pain hath passed away.

2 Well we know thy living faith,
Had the power to conquer death,

As a living rose may bloom,
By the border of the tomb.

3 Brother, in that solemn trust
We commend thee, dust to dust;
In that faith we wait, till risen,
Thou shalt meet us all in heaven.

* " *Or Sister.*'

41

76. What a Friend we have in Jesus.

UNKNOWN.   C. C. CONVERSE, by per.

1. What a friend we have in Je-sus, All our sins and griefs to bear; What a priv - i -
2. Have we tri -als and temp-ta-tions? Is there trouble a - nywhere? We should nev er
3. Are we weak and heav - y - la -den, Cumbered with a load of care; Precious Sav-iour,

lege to car-ry Ev-ery thing to God in prayer. Oh, what peace we oft - en for - feit,
be discouraged, Take it to the Lord in prayer. Can we find a friend so faith-ful,
still our refuge, Take it to the Lord in prayer. Do thy friends despise, forsake thee,

Oh, what needless pain we bear;—All because we do not carry Ev-ery thing to God in prayer.
Who will all our sorrows share; Jesus knows our every weakness, Take it to the Lord in prayer.
Take it to the Lord in prayer; In His arms He'll take and shield thee, Thou wilt find a solace there.

77. THE LOVE OF GOD.
Tune—WHAT A FRIEND.

1 THERE's a wideness in God's mercy,
  Like the wideness of the sea;
There's a kindness in His justice,
  Which is more than liberty.
There is welcome for the sinner,
  And more graces for the good;
There is mercy with the Saviour;
  There is healing in His blood.

2 There is no place where earth's sorrows
  Are more felt than up in heaven;
There is no place where earth's failings
  Have such kindly judgment given.

There is plentiful redemption
  In the blood that has been shed;
There is joy for all the members
  In the sorrows of the Head.

3 For the love of God is broader
  Than the measure of man's mind;
And the heart of the Eternal
  Is most wonderfully kind.
If our love were but more simple,
  We should take Him at His word;
And our lives would be all sunshine
  In the sweetness of our Lord.

Rev. F. W. Faber.

78. Bearing precious Seed in Love.

Dr. Thos. Hastings.   (STOCKWELL.)   Darius E. Jones.

1. He that go-eth forth with weeping, Bearing precious seed in love, Never tir-ing, nev-er
2. Soft descend the dews of heaven, Bright the rays celestial shine; Precious fruits will thus be

sleep-ing, Find-eth mer-cy from a - bove.
giv - en, Thro' an influence all di - vine.

3 Sow thy seed, be never weary,
  Let no fears thy soul annoy;
Be the prospect ne'er so dreary
  Thou shalt reap the fruits of joy.

4 Lo, the scene of verdure brightening'
  See the rising grain appear;
Look again! the fields are whitening,
  For the harvest time is near.

79. Jesus, the very thought of Thee.

Tr. by E. Caswell.   (HEBER.)   Geo. Kingsley.

1. Je - sus, the ve - ry thought of Thee, With sweetness fills my breast; But sweeter far Thy
2. Nor voice can sing, nor heart can frame, Nor can the memory find A sweeter sound than
3. O Hope of ev - ery contrite heart! O Joy of all the meek! To those who fall, how

face to see And in Thy presence rest.
Thy blest name. O Saviour of man - kind.
kind Thou art! How good to those who seek. A - men.

4 But what to those who find? Ah! this,
  Nor tongue nor pen can show;
The love of Jesus what it is,
  None but His loved ones know.

5 Jesus, our only joy be Thou,
  As thou our prize wilt be;
Jesus, be Thou our glory now,
  And through eternity.

80.   JESUS' NAME.

1 How SWEET the name of Jesus sounds
  In a believer's ear!
It soothes his sorrows, heals his wounds,
  And drives away his fear.

2 It makes the wounded spirit whole,
  And calms the troubled breast;
'T is manna to the hungry soul.
  And to the weary, rest.

3 Weak is the effort of my heart,
  And cold my warmest thought;
But when I see Thee as Thou art,
  I 'll praise Thee as I ought.

4 Till then I would Thy love proclaim,
  With every fleeting breath;
And may the music of Thy name,
  Refresh my soul in death.

Rev. John Newton.

81. Trusting Jesus, that is All.

Rev. EDGAR PAGE.　　　　　　　　　　　　　　IRA D. SANKEY, by per.

1. Simp - ly trusting ev - ery day, Trusting thro' a stormy way; Even when my faith is small,
2. Brightly doth His Spir-it shine In - to this poor heart of mine; While He leads I cannot fall,

CHORUS.

Trusting Je - sus, that is all. Trusting as the moments fly, Trusting as the days go by;
Trusting Je - sus, that is all.

Trusting Him whate'er befall, Trusting Jesus, that is all.

3 Singing, if my way is clear;
Praying, if the path be drear;
If in danger for Him call;
Trusting Jesus, that is all.

4 Trusting Him while life shall last,
Trusting Him till earth is past;
Till within the jasper wall,
Trusting Jesus, that is all.

82. Come, said Jesus' Sacred Voice.

A. L. BARBAULD.　　　　　(HORTON.)　　　　XAVIER SCHNYDER.

1. Come, said Jesus' sacred voice, Come, and make my path your choice; I will guide you to your
2. Thou, who, houseless, sole, forlorn,
Long hast borne the world's proud scorn,
Long hast roam'd the barren

home, Weary pilgrim, hith-er come!
waste, Weary pilgrim, hith-er haste.　A - men.

3 Ye who, tossed on beds of pain,
Seek for ease, but seek in vain;
Ye, by fiercer anguish torn,
In remorse for guilt who mourn;—

4 Hither come! for here is found
Balm and flowers for every wound,
Peace that ever shall endure,
Rest eternal, sacred, sure.

83. Holy Spirit, Faithful Guide.

M. M. WELLS, (1815—) 1858.　　　　　　　　MARCUS MORRIS WELLS.

1. Ho-ly Spir-it, faith-ful guide, Ev-er near the Christian's side; Gently lead us by the hand,
D. C. *Whisp'ring softly, wanderer come;*

Pilgrims in a des-ert land; Weary souls fore'er rejoice, While they hear that sweetest [voice.
Follow me, I'll guide thee home. A-MEN.

2 Ever present, truest Friend,
Ever near Thine aid to lend,
Leave us not to doubt and fear,
Groping on in darkness drear;
When the storms are raging sore,
Hearts grow faint, and hopes give o'er,
Whisper softly, wanderer come!
Follow me, I'll guide thee home.

3 When our days of toil shall cease,
Waiting still for sweet release,
Nothing left but heaven and prayer,
Wond'ring if our names were there;
Wading deep the dismal flood,
Pleading nought but Jesus' blood,
Whisper softly, wanderer come!
Follow me, I'll guide thee home!

84. MORE LIKE JESUS.

1 MORE like Jesus would I be,
Let my Saviour dwell with me;
Fill my soul with peace and love—
Make me gentle as a dove;
More like Jesus, while I go,
Pilgrim in this world below;
Poor in spirit would I be,
Let my Saviour dwell in me.

2 If He hears the raven's cry,
If His ever watchful eye
Marks the sparrows when they fall,
Surely He will hear my call.

He will teach me how to live,
All my sinful thoughts forgive;
Pure in heart I still would be—
Let my Saviour dwell in me.

3 More like Jesus when I pray,
More like Jesus day by day,
May I rest me by His side,
Where the tranquil waters glide.
Born of Him through grace renewed,
By His love my will subdued,
Rich in faith I still would be—
Let my Saviour dwell in me.

　　　　　Fanny J. Crosby.

85. GLORY TO GOD.

1 GLORY to the Father give,
God in whom we move and live:
Children's prayers He deigns to hear,
Children's songs delight His ear.
Glory to the Son we bring,
Christ our Prophet, Priest and King:
Children, raise your sweetest strain
To the Lamb, for He was slain.

2 Glory to the Holy Ghost,
He reclaims the sinner lost;
Children's minds may He inspire,
Touch their tongues with holy fire.
Glory in the highest be
To the Blessèd Trinity
For the Gospel from above,
For the word that "God is love."

James Montgomery.

86.

The Old, Old Story.

KATE HANKEY, 1867. W. H. DOANE, by per.

1. Tell me the old, old sto - ry Of un-seen things a - bove, Of Je - sus and His
2. Tell me the sto - ry slow-ly, That I may take it in— That wonder - ful re -
3. Tell me the same old sto - ry, When you have cause to fear That this world's empty

glo - ry Of Je - sus and His love. Tell me the sto - ry simply, As to a lit - tle
demption, God's rem-e - dy for sin. Tell me the sto - ry often, For I for-get so
glo - ry Is costing me too dear. Yes, and when that world's glory Is dawning on my

child, For I am weak and wea-ry, And help-less and de - filed. Tell me the old, old
soon! The "ear-ly dew" of morning Has pass'd a - way at noon.
soul, Tell me the old, old sto-ry, "Christ Je - sus makes thee whole."

CHORUS.

sto-ry, Tell me the old, old sto-ry, Tell me the old, old sto - ry Of Je-sus and His love.

87. I Love to Tell the Story.

KATE HANKEY, 1867.

WM. G. FISCHER. 1869, by per.

1. I love to tell the sto - ry; Of unseen things above, Of Je-sus and His glo-ry
2. I love to tell the sto - ry; More won-der-ful it seems Than all the golden fancies
3. I love to tell the sto - ry; 'Tis pleasant to repeat What seems, each time I tell it,
4. I love to tell the sto - ry; For those who know it best Seem hungering and thirsting

Of Je - sus and His love. I love to tell the sto - ry, Because I know it's true;
Of all our golden dreams. I love to tell the sto - ry; It did so much for me!
More wonder-ful - ly sweet. I love to tell the sto - ry; For some have nev-er heard
To hear it like the rest. And when, in scenes of glory, I sing the New, New Song,

CHORUS.

It sat - is-fies my longings, As nothing else can do. I love to tell the sto - ry,
And that is just the reason I tell it now to thee.
The message of sal - va-tion From God's own holy word.
'Twill be the Old, Old Sto-ry That I have loved so long.

'Twill be my theme in glo-ry, To tell the old, old sto-ry Of Je-sus and His love.

47

88.   # Safely through another Week.

REV. JOHN NEWTON.   LOWELL MASON, Mus. Doc.

1. Safe - ly through an - oth - er week, God has brought us on our way;
2. While we seek sup - plies of grace, Through the dear Re - deem - er's name,
3. Here we come Thy name to praise; Let us feel Thy pres - ence near:
4. May Thy gos - pel's joy - ful sound Con - quer sin - ners, com - fort saints;

Let us now a bless - ing seek, Wait - ing in His courts to - day:
Show Thy re - con - cil - ing face— Take a - way our sin and shame;
May Thy glo - ry meet our eyes, While we in Thy house ap - pear:
Make the fruits of grace a - bound, Bring re - lief for all com - plaints:

Day of all the week the best, Em - blem of e - ter - nal rest,
From our world - ly cares set free,— May we rest this day in Thee,
Here af - ford us, Lord, a taste Of our ev - er - last - ing feast.
Thus let all our Sab - baths prove, Till we rest in Thee a - bove.

Day of all the week the best, Em - blem of e - ter - nal rest.
From our world - ly cares set free,— May we rest this day in Thee.
Here af - ford us, Lord, a taste Of our ev - er - last - ing feast.
Thus let all our Sab - baths prove, Till we rest in Thee a - bove.

How Much I Owe.

Rev. Robert McCheyne.
(HALLE.)
Peter Ritter

1. { When this pass - ing world is done, When has sunk yon glo - rious sun;
   { When, from off the mount of God, We re - view the path we've trod;

2. { When I stand be - fore the throne, Clothed in beau - ty not my own;
   { When I see Thee as Thou art, Love Thee with un - sin - ning heart;

3. { When the praise of heaven I hear, Loud as thun-ders to the ear,
   { Loud as ma - ny wa - ters' noise, Sweet as harps' me-lodious voice,

Then, Lord, shall I ful - ly know— Not till then, how much I owe.
Then, Lord, shall I ful - ly know— Not till then, how much I owe.
Then, Lord, shall I ful - ly know— Not till then, how much I owe.

90.

1 CHRIST, whose glory fills the skies,
   Christ, the true, the only Light,
Sun of Righteousness, arise,
   Triumph o'er the shades of night;
Day-spring from on high be near,
Day-star, in my heart appear.

2 Dark and cheerless is the morn,
   Unaccompanied by Thee;
Joyless is the day's return,
   Till Thy mercy's beams I see,
Till they inward light impart,
Glad my eyes, and warm my heart.

Visit, then, this soul of mine;
   Pierce the gloom of sin and grief;
Fill me, Radiancy divine,
   Scatter all my unbelief;
More and more Thyself display,
Shining to the perfect day!
Rev. Chas. Wesley.

91.

1 THEY who seek the throne of grace
   Find that throne in every place,
   If we live a life of prayer,
   God is present everywhere.

2 In our sickness and our health,
   In our want, or in our wealth,
   If we look to God in prayer,
   God is present everywhere.

3 When our earthly comforts fail,
   When the woes of life prevail,
   'Tis the time for earnest prayer;
   God is present everywhere.

4 Then, my soul, in every strait,
   To thy Father come, and wait;
   He will answer every prayer:
   God is present everywhere.
Oliver Holden, alt.

92.   I heard the Voice of Jesus say.

HORATIUS BONAR, D. D. 1850.   FRANZ ABT. Arr. by H. P. MAIN.

SOLO OR DUET.   CHORUS.

1. I heard the voice of Je - sus say, "Come, un - to me and rest;
2. I heard the voice of Je - sus say, "Be - hold, I free - ly give
3. I heard the voice of Je - sus say, "I am this dark world's light;

SOLO OR DUET.   CHORUS.

Lay down, thou wea - ry one, lay down Thy head up - on my breast."
The liv - ing wa - ter; thirst - y one, Stoop down and drink, and live."
Look un - to me, thy morn shall rise, And all thy day be bright."

FULL CHORUS.

I came to Je - sus as I was, Wea - ry, and worn, and sad,......
I came to Je - sus, and I drank Of that life-giv - ing stream,...
I looked to Je - sus, and I found In Him my Star, my Sun,......

I found in Him a rest - ing place, And He, and He has made me glad.
My thirst was quenched, my soul re - vived, And now, and now I live in Him.
And in that light of life I'll walk, Till all, till all my days are done.

50

93. We shall Meet By and By.

JOHN ATKINSON, D.D. 1867.   HUBERT P. MAIN, by per.

1. We shall meet be-yond the riv-er, By and by, by and by;
2. We shall strike the harps of glo-ry, By and by, by and by;

And the dark-ness will be o-ver, By and by, by and by;
We shall sing re-demption's sto-ry, By and by, by and by;

With the toil-some jour-ney done, And the glo-rious bat-tle won,
And the strains for-ev-er-more Shall re-sound in sweetness o'er,

We shall shine forth as the sun, By and by, by and by.
Yon-der ev-er-last-ing shore, By and by, by and by.

3 We shall see and be like Jesus,
   By and by, by and by;
Who a crown of life will give us,
   By and by, by and by;
And the angels who fulfil
All the mandates of His will
Shall attend, and love us still,
   By and by, by and by.

4 Wearing robes of snowy whiteness,
   By and by, by and by;
And with crowns of dazzling brightness,
   By and by, by and by;
Then, our storms and perils passed,
And with glory ours at last,
We'll possess the kingdom vast,
   By and by, by and by.

94. Come, we who Love the Lord.

ISAAC WATTS. (ST. THOMAS.) HANDEL. A. Williams' Coll.

1. Come, we who love the Lord, And let our joys be known;
2. Let those re - fuse to sing Who nev - er knew our God;
3. The men of grace have found Glo - ry be - gun be - low;

Join in a song of sweet ac - cord, And thus surround the throne.
But chil - dren of the heavenly King May speak their joys a - broad.
Ce - les - tial fruits on earth - ly ground From faith and hope may grow. *Amen.*

4 The hill of Zion yields
  A thousand sacred sweets,
Before we reach the heavenly fields,
  Or walk the golden streets.

5 Then let our songs abound,
  And every tear be dry;
We're marching through Immanuel's ground
  To fairer worlds on high.

95.

1 WELCOME, sweet day of rest,
  That saw the Lord arise!
Welcome to this reviving breast,
  And these rejoicing eyes!

2 The King himself comes near,
  And feasts his saints to-day;
Here may we sit and see Him here,
  And love, and praise, and pray.

3 One day, amid the place
  Where my dear Lord hath been,
Is sweeter than ten thousand days
  Within the tents of sin.

4 My willing soul would stay
  In such a frame as this,
And sit and sing herself away
  To everlasting bliss.

Isaac Watts.

96. How gentle God's Commands!

P. DODDRIDGE, D.D. (DENNIS.) H. G. NÄGELI. arr. by W. B. BRADBURY.

1. How gen - tle God's commands! How kind His pre - cepts are!
2. Be - neath His watch - ful eye His saints se - cure - ly dwell;
3. Why should this anx - ious load Press down your wea - ry mind?
4. His good - ness stands ap - proved, Un - changed from day to day:

How gentle God's Commands!—Concluded.

Come, cast your bur - dens on the Lord, And trust His con-stant care.
That hand which bears cre - a - tion up Shall guard His chil - dren well.
Haste to your heaven-ly Father's throne, And sweet re-freshment find.
I'll drop my bur - den at His feet, And bear a song a - way. A - *men.*

97.

1 LIKE Noah's weary dove,
   That soared the earth around;
But not a resting-place above
   The cheerless waters found.

2 O cease, my wand'ring soul,
   On restless wings to roam;
All the wide world, to either pole,
   Has not for thee a home.

3 Behold the Ark of God,
   Behold the open door !

Hasten to gain that dear abode,
   And rove, my soul, no more.

4 There, safe thou shalt abide,
   There sweet shall be thy rest,
And every longing satisfied,
   With full salvation blest.

5 And when the waves of ire,
   Again the earth shall fill,
The Ark shall ride the sea of fire,
   Then rest on Sion's hill.
                           W. A. Muhlenberg, D.D.

98.   Lead Me On.

ANON.   C. C. CONVERSE, by per.

1. Traveling to the bet - ter land, O'er the desert's scorching sand, Fa-ther! let me
2. When at Ma-rah, parched with heat, I the sparkling fountain greet, Make the bit - ter
3. When the wil-der-ness is drear, Show me Elim's palm-grove near, And her wells, as
4. Thro' the wa-ter, thro' the fire, Nev - er let me fall or tire, Ev-ery step brings

grasp Thy hand, Lead me   on, lead me   on.
wa - ter sweet, Lead me   on, lead me   on.
crys - tal clear, Lead me on, lead me   on.
Ca-naan nigher, Lead me   on, lead me   on.

5 Bid me stand on Nebo's height,
   Gaze upon the land of light,
   Then, transported with the sight,
      Lead me on !

6 When I stand on Jordan's brink,
   Never let me fear or shrink;
   Hold me, Father, lest I sink:
      Lead me on !

7 When the victory is won,
   And eternal life begun,
   Up to glory lead me on !
      Lead me on !

99. The Rock that is Higher than I.

W. G. FISCHER, by per.

1. Oh, sometimes the shadows are deep, And rough seems the path to the goal, And sorrows some-
2. Oh, sometimes how long seems the day, And sometimes how weary my feet; But toil-ing in
3. Oh, near to the Rock let me keep, If blessings, or sorrows pre-vail; Or climbing the

CHORUS.

times how they sweep, Like tempests down o-ver the soul. Oh, then, to the Rock let me
life's dusty way, The Rock's blessed shadow how sweet. Oh, then, to the Rock let me
mountain way steep, Or walk-ing the sha-dow-y vale. Then, quick to the Rock I can

fly, let me fly, To the Rock that is high-er than I: Oh,
fly, let me fly, To the Rock that is high-er than I: Oh,
fly, I can fly, To the Rock that is high-er than I: Then,

is high-er than I,

then to the Rock let me fly, let me fly, To the Rock that is high-er than I.
then to the Rock let me fly, let me fly, To the Rock that is high-er than I.
quick to the Rock I can fly, I can fly, To the Rock that is high-er than I.

100. We Speak of the Realms of the Blest.

Mrs. Elizabeth Mills.   J. C. Engelbrecht.

1. We speak, we speak of the realms of the blest, Of that country so bright and so fair;
2. We speak, we speak of its pathways of gold, Of its walls deck'd with jewels most rare,

D.S.

And oft are its glo-ries confessed, confessed; But what must it be to be there?
Its won-ders and pleasures un-told, un - told; But what must it be to be there?

REFRAIN.

But what must it be to be there?

3 We speak, we speak of its freedom from sin,
  From sorrow, temptation, and care,
  From trials without, and from trials within—
  But what must it be to be there?

4 Do Thou, do Thou, Lord, 'midst pleasure or
    woe,
  For heaven our spirits prepare;
  Then soon shall we joyfully know, yes, know,
  And feel what it is to be there.

101. Gentle Shepherd, grant Thy Blessing.

GERMAN.

1. Gen-tle Shepherd, grant Thy blessing On us now, While be-fore Thy throne we bow.
2. Gen-tle Shepherd, we Thy children Seek Thy face: Give us now Thy heavenly grace.
3. Gen-tle Shepherd, when life's ended, Take us home, Nev- er from Thy side to roam.

102. Rock of Ages.

Rev. A. M. Toplady.

Franz Abt, arr. by H. P. Main.

1. Rock of a - ges, cleft for me, Let me hide myself in Thee! Let the wa-ter and the blood,
2. Not the la-bors of my hands Can fulfill Thy law's demands: Could my zeal no respite know,
3. Noth-ing in my hand I bring: Simply to Thy cross I cling; Naked, come to Thee for dress,
4. While I draw this fleeting breath, When my eyelids close in death, When I soar to worlds unknown,

DUET.

From Thy wounded side which flow'd, Be of sin the perfect cure, Cleanse me from its guilt and pow'r.
Could my tears forev - er flow, All for sin could not a-tone: Thou must save, and Thou a - lone.
Helpless, look to Thee for grace; Foul, I to Thy fountain fly; Wash me, Saviour, or I die.
See Thee on Thy judgment throne, Rock of A - ges, cleft for me, Let me hide myself in Thee.

WHOLE SCHOOL.

rit.

Rock of A - ges, cleft for me, Let me hide myself in Thee; Let me hide myself in Thee.

103. Rock of Ages. 7s. 6 lines.

Thos. Hastings.

1. Rock of A - ges, cleft for me! Let me hide myself in Thee; Let the wa - ter and the blood,
2. While I draw this fleeting breath, When my eyelids close in death, When I soar to worlds unknown,

58

Rock of Ages.—Concluded.

From Thy wounded side that flow'd, Be of sin the double cure; Cleanse me from its guilt and pow'r.
See Thee on Thy judgment throne, Rock of A - ges, cleft for me! Let me hide myself in Thee.

104. Saviour, Like a Shepherd lead us.

Miss DOROTHY ANN THRUPP, 1836.   WILLIAM B. BRADBURY. by per.

1. Sav-iour, like a shepherd lead us, Much we need Thy tender care; In Thy pleasant pastures
2. We are Thine, do Thou befriend us, Be the guardian of our way; Keep Thy flock, from sin de-

feed us, For our use Thy folds prepare, Blessed Je-sus, Blessed Je-sus, Thou hast
fend us, Seek us when we go a - stray; Blessed Je-sus, Blessed Je-sus, Hear the

bought us, Thine we are, Blessed Je-sus, Blessed Je-sus, Thou hast bought us, Thine we are.
children when they pray, Blessed Je-sus, Blessed Je-sus, Hear the children when they pray.

Copyrighted, 1859, in The Oriola, by W. B. Bradbury.

3 Thou hast promised to receive us,
　Poor and sinful though we be;
　Thou hast mercy to relieve us,
　　Grace to cleanse, and power to free;
　　Blessed Jesus,
　Let us early turn to Thee.

4 Early let us seek Thy favor,
　Early let us do Thy will;
　Holy Lord, our only Saviour,
　　With Thy grace our bosoms fill;
　　Blessed Jesus,
　Thou hast loved us, love us still.

105. Father of Love, our Guide and Friend.

Rev. Wm. J. Irons.   (LAUD.)   Rev. John B. Dykes, 1861.

1. Fa - ther of love, our Guide and Friend, Oh, lead us gen - tly on,
2. We know not what the path may be, As yet by us un - trod;
3. If call'd, like Abraham's child to climb The hill of sac - ri - fice;

Un - til life's tri - al - time shall end, And heav - enly peace be won.
But we can trust our all to Thee, Our Fa - ther and our God.
Some an - gel may be there in time, De - liv - erance shall a - rise. A - men.

4 Or if some darker lot be good,
   Oh, teach us to endure
The sorrow, pain, and solitude,
   That make the spirit pure.

5 Christ by no flowery pathway came,
   And we His followers here,
Must do Thy will, and praise Thy name,
   In hope, and love, and fear.

106.

1 Speak gently, it is better far
   To rule by love than fear;
Speak gently: let no harsh word mar
   The good we may do here.

2 Speak gently to the erring: know
   They must have toiled in vain;
Perchance unkindness made them so;
   O win them back again.

3 Speak gently: 'tis a little thing,
   Dropped in the heart's deep well;

The good, the joy that it may bring,
   Eternity shall tell.

107.

1 I worship Thee, sweet Will of God,
   And all Thy ways adore;
And every day I live, I seem
   To love Thee more and more.

2 When obstacles and trials seem
   Like prison walls to be,
I do the little I can do,
   And leave the rest to Thee.

3 He always wins who sides with God,
   To him no chance is lost;
God's will is sweetest to him when
   It triumphs at his cost.

4 Ill that He blesses is our good,
   And unblest good is ill;
And all is right that seems most wrong,
   If it be His sweet will!

58   Rev. F. W. Faber.

108. Love of the Unseen Lord.

Rev. Ray Palmer, D. D. tr.   (SOUTHPORT.)   Geo. Kingsley.

1. Je - sus, these eyes have never seen That radiant form of Thine! The veil of sense hangs
2. I see Thee not, I hear Thee not, Yet art Thou oft with me; And earth hath ne'er so
3. Like some bright dream that comes unsought, When slumbers o'er me roll, Thine image ever

dark between Thy blessed face and mine!
dear a spot, As where I meet with Thee.
fills my thought, And charms my ravished soul. *Amen.*

4 Yet though I have not seen, and still
   Must rest in faith alone;
  I love Thee, dearest Lord!—and will,
   Unseen, but not unknown.

5 When death these mortal eyes shall seal,
   And still this throbbing heart,
  The rending veil shall Thee reveal,
   All glorious as Thou art!

109. Nearer, my God, to Thee.

Sarah F. Adams.   (BETHANY.)   Lowell Mason by per.

1. Near-er, my God, to Thee! Nearer, to Thee, Ev'n tho' it be a cross That raiseth me;
2. Tho', like a wan-der-er, The sun gone down, Darkness be o - ver me, My rest a stone,
3. There let the way appear, Steps un-to heav'n; All that Thou sendest me, In mercy given;
4. Then, with my waking thoughts Bright with Thy praise, Out of my stony griefs Bethel I'll raise;

Still all my song shall be, Nearer, my God, to Thee, Nearer, my God, to Thee, Nearer to Thee!
Yet in my dreams I'd be Nearer, my God, to Thee, Nearer, my God, to Thee, Nearer to Thee!
An - gels to beckon me Nearer, my God, to Thee, Nearer, my God, to Thee, Nearer to Thee!
So by my woes to be Nearer, my God, to Thee, Nearer, my God, to Thee, Nearer to Thee!

110. He Leadeth Me.

Prof. Jos. H. Gilmore, 1861. Wm. B. Bradbury, by per.

1. He lead - eth me! oh! bless - ed thought, Oh! words with heavenly comfort fraught;
2. Sometimes 'mid scenes of deep - est gloom, Sometimes where E - den's bowers bloom,

What-e'er I do, wher-e'er I be, Still 'tis God's hand that lead - eth me.
By wa - ters still, o'er troubled sea,— Still 'tis His hand that lead - eth me.

REFRAIN.

He lead-eth me! He lead - eth me! By His own hand He lead-eth me;

His faith - ful follower I would be, For by His hand He lead-eth me.

3 Lord, I would clasp Thy hand in mine,
Nor ever murmur nor repine—
Content, whatever lot I see,
Since 'tis my God that leadeth me.

4 And when my task on earth is done,
When, by Thy grace, the victory's won,
E'en death's cold wave I will not flee,
Since God through Jordan leadeth me.

111.   Jesus, Engrave it on my Heart.

SAMUEL MEDLEY, 1789.   (EVENING HYMN.)   THOS. TALLIS.

1. Je - sus, en-grave it on my heart That Thou the one thing need - ful art;

I could from all things parted be, But nev-er, nev - er, Lord, from Thee. Amen.

2 Needful is Thy most precious blood
To reconcile my soul to God,
Needful is Thy indulgent care,
Needful Thy all-prevailing prayer.

3 Needful Thy presence, dearest Lord,
True peace and comfort to afford,
Needful Thy promise, to impart
Fresh life and vigor to my heart.

4 Needful art Thou, my Guide, my Stay,
Through all life's dark and weary way;
Nor less in death Thou'lt needful be
To bring my spirit home to Thee.

5 Then needful still, my God, my King,
Thy name eternally I'll sing!
Glory and praise be ever His—
The one thing needful Jesus is!

112.

1 GLORY to Thee, my God this night,
For all the blessings of the light;
Keep me, oh, keep me, King of kings!
Beneath Thine own almighty wings.

2 Forgive me, Lord, for Thy dear Son,
The ill which I this day have done;
That with the world, myself, and Thee,
I, ere I sleep, at peace may be.

3 Teach me to live, that I may dread
The grave as little as my bed:
Teach me to die, that so I may
Rise glorious at the judgment-day.

4 Oh, let my soul on Thee repose,
And may sweet sleep mine eyelids close!
Sleep, which shall me more vigorous make,
To serve my God when I awake.

Thos. Ken.

113.

1 Now LET my soul, eternal King,
To Thee its grateful tribute bring;
My knee with humble homage bow,
My tongue perform its solemn vow.

2 All nature sings Thy boundless love,
In worlds below and worlds above;
But in Thy blessed word I trace
Diviner wonders of Thy grace.

3 Here Jesus bids my sorrows cease,
And gives my laboring conscience peace;
Here lifts my grateful passions high,
And points to mansions in the sky.

4 For love like this, oh, let my song,
Through endless years, Thy praise prolong;
Let distant climes Thy name adore,
Till time and nature are no more.

O. Heginbotham

114. Around the Throne.

Mrs. ANNIE H. SHEPHERD.　　　　　　　　　HENRY E. MATHEWS.

1. Around the throne of God in heav'n, Thousands of children stand; Children whose sins are all for-
2. In flowing robes of spotless white, See ev - ery one arrayed; Dwelling in ev - er - last-ing
3. What bro't them to that world above? That heav'n so bright and fair, Where all is peace, and joy, and

given; A ho - ly, happy band, Singing glo-ry, glo - ry, glo - ry be to God on high.
light, And joys that nev-er fade, Singing glo-ry, glo - ry, glo - ry be to God on high.
love, —How came those children there? Singing glory, &c.

4 Because the Saviour shed His blood,
　　To wash away their sin;
　Bathed in that pure and precious flood,
　　Behold them white and clean!
　　Singing glory, &c.

5 On earth they sought the Saviour's grace,
　　On earth they loved His name;
　So now they see His blessed face,
　　And stand before the Lamb,
　　Singing glory, &c.

115. The Hour of Prayer.

CHARLOTTE ELLIOTT.　　　　　(URMUND.)　　　　LOWELL MASON, 1832.

1. My God, is a - ny hour so sweet, From blush of morn to evening star, As that which
2. Then is my strength by Thee renewed; Then are my sins by Thee forgiven; Then dost Thou

calls me to Thy feet, As that which calls me to Thy feet, The hour of prayer.
cheer my sol - i - tude Then dost Thou cheer my sol - i - tude With hopes of heaven. Amen.

62

The Hour of Prayer.—Concluded.

3 No words can tell what blest relief
 There for my every want I find;
What strength for warfare, balm for grief;
 What peace of mind.

4 Hushed is each doubt; gone every fear,
 My spirit seems in heaven to stay;

And e'en the penitential tear
 Is wiped away.

5 Lord, till I reach yon blissful shore,
 No privilege so dear shall be,
As thus my inmost soul to pour
 In prayer to Thee:

116.   Joy to the world,—the Lord has come.

ISAAC WATTS.   (ANTIOCH.)   LOWELL MASON, arr.

1. Joy to the world—the Lord has come; Let earth re-ceive her King,
2. Joy to the earth,—the Sav-iour reigns; Let men their songs em-ploy;

Let ev-ery heart pre-pare Him room, And heav'n and na-ture sing, And
While fields and floods, rocks, hills and plains, Re-peat the sounding joy, Re-

And heav'n and nature
Re - peat the sounding

heav'n and na-ture sing,................ And heav'n and na-ture sing.
peat the sounding joy,................ Re-peat the sounding joy. A-men.

sing.   And heav'n and nature   sing.
joy,   Re - peat the sounding   joy.

3 No more let sin and sorrow grow,
 Nor thorns infest the ground,
He comes to make His blessings flow.
 Far as the curse is found.

4 He rules the world with truth and grace,
 And makes the nations prove
The glories of His righteousness,
 And wonders of His love.

117. **Beauteous Day.**

Rev. Wm. O. Cushing.   Geo. F. Root, 1866.

Slow.

1. We are watching, we are waiting, For the bright, prophet-ic day: When the shadows,
2. We are watching, we are waiting, For the star that brings the day: When the night of
3. We are watching, we are waiting, For the beauteous King of day: For the Chiefest

CHORUS.

wea - ry shadows, From the world shall roll a - way. We are waiting for the morning,
sin shall vanish, And the shadows melt a - way.
of ten thousand, For the Light, the Truth, the Way.

When the beauteous day is dawning; We are waiting for the morning, For the

gold-en spires of day. Lo! He comes! see the King draw near; Zion, shout, the Lord is near.

Copyright by John Church & Co.

118. A GOOD TIME TO LIVE IN.

1 We are living, we are dwelling,
In a grand and awful time,
In an age on ages telling;
To be living is sublime.

2 Oh! let all the soul within you
For the truth's sake go abroad,
Strike, let every nerve and sinew
Tell on ages, tell for God.

Rev. Arthur Cleveland Coxe. (1818—) 1840.

64

119. There is no Name so Sweet.

Dr. Geo. W. Bethune, 1858.   Wm. B. Bradbury, by per.

1. There is no name so sweet on earth, No name so sweet in heaven, The name before His
2. And when He hung up - on the tree, They wrote this name above Him, That all might see the
3. So now, up - on His Father's throne, Al - mighty to re - lease us From sin and pains, He
4. O Je-sus! by that matchless name Thy grace shall fail us nev - er; To - day as yes - ter -

REFRAIN.

wondrous birth To Christ the Sav - iour giv - en. We love to sing around our King,
rea - son we For - ev - er - more must love Him.
ev - er reigns, The Prince and Sav-iour Je - sus.
day the same, Thou art the same for - ev - er.

And hail Him blessed Je - sus; For there's no word ear ever heard So dear, so sweet as "Jesus."

Copyright, 1861, in "Golden Chain."

120. CHRIST IS COMING.

Tune.—BEAUTEOUS DAY.

1 He is coming, He is coming,
   Not as once He came before,
   But upon His cloud of glory
   In the crimson-tinted sky.

2 He is coming, He is coming,
   Let His lowly first estate,

And His tender love, so teach us
   That in faith and hope we wait.

3 Till in glory eastward burning,
   Our redemption draweth near:
   And we see the sign in heaven
   Of our Judge and Saviour dear.

Cecil Frances Alexander, 1858.

65

121.
Sweet Hour of Prayer.

Rev. W. W. WALFORD, 1846.   WM. B. BRADBURY, by per.

Slow.

1. Sweet hour of prayer! sweet hour of prayer! That calls me from a world of care, And bids me

at my Fa-ther's throne, Make all my wants and wish-es known: In seasons of dis-

tress and grief, My soul has oft-en found re-lief; And oft escaped the tempter's snare, By

thy return, sweet hour of pray'r, And oft escaped the tempter's snare, By thy return, sweet hour of pray'r.

Copyrighted, 1869, by Wm. B. Bradbury.

2 Sweet hour of prayer! sweet hour of prayer!
Thy wings shall my petition bear
To Him whose truth and faithfulness
Engage the waiting soul to bless.
And since He bids me seek His face,
Believe His word, and trust His grace,
||:I'll cast on Him my every care
And wait for thee, sweet hour of prayer! :||

3 Sweet hour of prayer! sweet hour of prayer!
May I thy consolation share,
Till, from Mount Pisgah's lofty height,
I view my home and take my flight:
This robe of flesh I'll drop, and rise
To seize the everlasting prize;
||: And shout, while passing through the air,
Farewell, farewell, sweet hour of prayer! :||

122.   **Dear Saviour we are Thine.**

P. DODDRIDGE.   (GOLDEN HILL.)   A. DAVISSON.

1. Dear Sav-iour! we are Thine, By ev-er-last-ing bands; Our hearts, our
2. To Thee we still would cleave With ev-er-grow-ing zeal; If mil-lions

souls, we would re-sign En-tire-ly to Thy hands,
tempt us Christ to leave, Oh, let them ne'er pre-vail! A-men.

3 Thy Spirit shall unite
  Our souls to Thee, our Head;
Shall form in us Thine image bright,
  And teach Thy paths to tread.

4 Death may our souls divide
  From these abodes of clay;
But love shall keep us near Thy side,
  Through all the gloomy way.

5 Since Christ and we are one,
  Why should we doubt or fear?
If He in heaven has fixed His throne,
  He'll fix His members there.

123.

1 Not all the blood of beasts
  On Jewish altars slain,
Could give the guilty conscience peace,
  Or wash away the stain.

2 But Christ the heavenly Lamb
  Takes all our sins away,
A sacrifice of nobler name
  And richer blood than they.

3 My faith would lay her hand
  On that dear head of Thine,
While like a penitent I stand,
  And there confess my sin.

4 My soul looks back to see
  The burden Thou didst bear,
When hanging on the cursed tree,
  And hopes her guilt was there.

5 Believing we rejoice
  To see the curse remove;
We bless the Lamb with cheerful voice.
  And sing His dying love.

                    I. WATTS.

124.   REST IN JESUS.

1 My Spirit on Thy care
  Blest Saviour, I recline ;
Thou wilt not leave me to despair,
  For THOU art LOVE DIVINE.

2 In Thee I place my trust,
  On Thee I calmly rest ;
I know Thee good, I know Thee just,
  And count Thy choice the best.

3 Whate'er events betide,
  Thy will they all perform ;
Safe in Thy Breast my head I hide,
  Nor fear the coming storm.

4 Let good or ill befall,
  It must be good for me ;
Secure of having Thee in all,
  Of having All in Thee.

             Rev. Henry F. Lyte. 1834.

125. Forever with the Lord.

J. MONTGOMERY, alt.

I. B. WOODBURY, 1852.

1. For-ev - er with the Lord, So, Je - sus, let it be! Life from the dead is in that word, 'Tis

im - mor-tal - i - ty. Here in the body pent, Absent from Thee I roam, Yet nightly pitch my

moving tent, A day's march nearer home. Nearer home, nearer home, A day's march nearer home.

2 My Father's house on high,
Home of my soul, how near,
At times to faith's aspiring eye,
Thy golden gates appear.
Forever with the Lord,
Father, if 'tis Thy will,
The promise of Thy gracious word,
E'en here to me fulfil.
With the Lord, with the Lord,
Forever with the Lord.

3 So when my latest breath
Shall rend the vail in twain,
By death I shall escape from death,
And life eternal gain.
Knowing as I am known:
How shall I love that word,
And oft repeat before the throne,
Forever with the Lord.
With the Lord, with the Lord,
Forever with the Lord.

126. Forever with the Lord.

J. MONTGOMERY, alt.

(OLMUTZ.)

Adapted by LOWELL MASON.

1. "For - ev - er with the Lord!" So, Je - sus! let it be;

Life from the dead is in that word; 'Tis im - mor tal - i - ty.

127. I'll Enter the Open Door.

(THE MISTAKES OF MY LIFE.)

Mrs. URANIA LOOKE BAILEY.　　　　　　　　　　Rev. ROBERT LOWRY, by per.

Tenderly.

1. The mistakes of my life have been ma-ny, The sins of my heart have been
2. I am low-est of those who love Him, I am weak-est of those who
3. My mistakes His free grace will cov-er, My sins He will wash a-
4. The mistakes of my life have been ma-ny, And my spir-it is sick with

more, And I scarce can see for weeping, But I'll knock at the o-pen door.
pray; But I come as He has bid-den, And He will not say me nay.
way, And the feet that shrink and fal-ter Shall walk thro' the gates of day.
sin, And I scarce can see for weeping, But the Sav-iour will let me in.

CHORUS.

I know I am weak and sin-ful, It comes to me more and more; But

when the dear Saviour shall bid me come in, I'll en-ter the o-pen door.

128. Jesus, Saviour, Pilot Me.

Rev. EDWARD HOPPER, D. D., 1871. alt.   (PILOT.)   J. E. GOULD.

1. Je - sus, Sav - iour, pi - lot me, O - ver life's tem - pest - uous sea;
2. As a moth - er stills her child, Thou canst hush the o - cean wild;
3. When at last I near the shore, And the fear - ful break - ers roar

Un-known waves be - fore me roll, Hid - ing rock and treacherous shoal;
Boisterous waves o - bey Thy will When Thou say'st to them "Be still!"
'Twixt me and the peace - ful rest, Then, while lean - ing on Thy breast,

Chart and com - pass come from Thee: Je - sus, Sav - iour, pi - lot me.
Won-drous Sove-reign of the sea, Je - sus, Sav - iour, pi - lot me.
May I hear Thee say to me, "Fear not, I will pi - lot thee!"

129.   FATHER, LEAD ME.

1 FATHER, lead me, day by day,
Ever in Thine own sweet way;
Teach me to be pure and true,
Show me what I ought to do.
Keep me safe by Thy dear side;
Let me in Thy love abide.

2 When I'm tempted to do wrong,
Make me steadfast, wise, and strong;
And when all alone I stand,
Shield me with Thy mighty hand.
Happy most of all to know
That my Father loves me so,

3 When my work seems hard and dry,
May I press on cheerily;
May I do the good I know,
Be Thy loving child below,
Then at last go home to Thee,
Evermore Thy child to be

70

130. Light and Life from Thee, oh, Lord.

(HALLE.)

PETER RITTER.

1. Lord, Thy chil-dren guide and keep As with fee-ble steps they press,
2. There are ston-y ways to tread; Give the strength we sore-ly lack;

On the path-way rough and steep, Thro' this wea-ry wil-der-ness,
There are tan-gled paths to thread; Light us, lest we miss the track,

Ho-ly Je-sus, day by day, Lead us in the nar-row way.

3 There are sandy wastes that lie
  Cold and sunless, vast and drear,
Where the feeble faint and die;
  Grant us grace to persevere.
Holy Jesus, day by day,
Lead us in the narrow way.

4 There are soft and flowery glades
  Decked with golden-fruited trees,
Sunny slopes and scented shades:
  Keep us, Lord, from slothful ease.
Holy Jesus, day by day,
Lead us in the narrow way.

5 Upward still to purer heights,
  Onward yet to scenes more blest,
Calmer regions, clearer lights,
  Till we reach the promised rest.
Holy Jesus, day by day,
Lead us in the narrow way.

181. THE LIVING WORD.

1 SAVIOUR, on this little band,
  Gathered here to learn of Thee,

Now in blessing lay Thy hand;
  Touch our eyes that we may see,
Shining through Thy Holy Word,
  Light and life from Thee, O Lord!

2 From the bounty of Thy store
  Daily may our souls be fed;
Lest we hunger, evermore
  Give us of the heavenly bread;
May our souls be strong, O Lord!
  With the manna of Thy word.

3 With the water of Thy love
  Now our earthen pitchers fill,
Flowing from Thy throne above,
  Free to "whosoever will;"
From this fountain of Thy word
  We would drink and live, O Lord!

4 All our blessing comes from Thee,
  Christ, the living Word from heaven!
All our powers to do or be
  To Thy service shall be given:
May Thy presence with us still
  Make us wise to learn Thy will.

132. I am Trusting, Lord, in Thee.

Rev. Wm. McDonald, 1869.　　　　　　　　Wm. G. Fischer, 1869, by per.

1. I am com-ing to the cross; I am poor and weak and blind; I am counting all but

Cho.—I am trusting, Lord, in Thee, Dear Lamb of Cal-va-ry; Humbly at Thy cross I

dross; I shall full sal-va-tion find.

bow; Save me Je-sus, save me now.

2 Long my heart has sighed for Thee;
   Long has evil reigned within:
   Jesus sweetly speaks to me,
   I will cleanse you from all sin.

3 In Thy promises I trust;
   Now I feel the blood applied;
   I am prostrate in the dust;
   I with Christ am crucified.

133. In the Cross of Christ I Glory

Sir John Bowring, 1825.　　　(RATHBUN.)　　　Ithamar Conkey, 1849.

1. In the cross of Christ I glo-ry, Towering o'er the wrecks of time;
2. When the woes of life o'ertake me, Hopes de-ceive and fears an-noy,

All the light of sa-cred sto-ry Gathers round its head sub-lime.
Nev-er shall the cross for-sake me; Lo! it glows with peace and joy. A-men.

3 When the sun of bliss is beaming
   Light and love upon my way,
   From the cross the radiance streaming
   Adds more lustre to the day.

4 Bane and blessing, pain and pleasure,
   By the cross are sanctified;
   Peace is there that knows no measure,
   Joys that through all times abide.

134. O could I speak the Matchless Worth.

S. MEDLEY.   (ARIEL.)   MOZART. Arr. by LOWELL MASON.

1. Oh, could I speak the match-less worth, O could I sound the glo-ries forth,
2. I'd sing the pre-cious blood He spilt, My ran-som from the dreadful guilt,
3. I'd sing the char-ac-ters He bears, And all the forms of love He wears,

Which in my Saviour shine! I'd soar, and touch the heav'nly strings And vie with Gabriel
Of sin and wrath di-vine! I'd sing His glorious righteousness In which all-per-fect
Ex-alt-ed on His throne; In loft-iest songs of sweetest praise, I would to ev-er-

while He sings In notes al-most di-vine, In notes al-most di-vine.
heavenly dress My soul shall ev-er shine, My soul shall ev-er shine.
last-ing days Make all His glo-ries known, Make all His glo-ries known. A-men.

4 Well—the delightful day will come,
  When my dear Lord will bring me home,
    And I shall see His face:
  Then with my Saviour, Brother, Friend,
  A blest eternity I'll spend,
    Triumphant in His grace.

135.

1 Come join, ye saints, with heart and voice,
  Alone in Jesus to rejoice,
    And worship at His feet;
  Come, take His praises on your tongues,
  And raise to Him your thankful songs,
    "In Him ye are complete!"

2 In Him, who all our praise excels,
  The fullness of the Godhead dwells,
    And all perfections meet:
  The head of all celestial powers,
  Divinely theirs, divinely ours ;—
    "In Him ye are complete!"

3 Still onward urge your heavenly way,
  Dependent on Him day by day,
    His presence still entreat;
  His precious name for ever bless,
  Your glory, strength, and righteousness,
    "In Him ye are complete!"

136. **Jesus, Lover of my Soul.**

Rev. C. WESLEY.   (REFUGE.)   J. P. HOLBROOK, by per.

CHOIR.

1. Je - sus! lov - er of my soul, Let me to Thy bo - som fly
2. Oth - er ref - uge have I none; Hangs my help - less soul on Thee;
3. Thou, O Christ! art all I want; More than all in Thee I find;
4. Plenteous grace with Thee is found,— Grace to par - don all my sin;

While the bil - lows near me roll, While the tem - pest still is high;
Leave, ah! leave me not a - lone, Still sup - port and com - fort me.
Raise the fall - en, cheer the faint, Heal the sick, and lead the blind.
Let the heal - ing streams abound, Make and keep me pure with - in;

CONGREGATION.

Hide me, O my Saviour! hide, Till the storm of life is past;
All my trust on Thee is stayed; All my help from Thee I bring;
Just and ho - ly is Thy name, I am all un - righteous - ness;
Thou of life the foun - tain art, Free - ly let me take of Thee;

Safe in - to the ha - ven guide; Oh, re - ceive my soul at last!
Cov - er my de - fence-less head With the shad - ow of Thy wing.
Vile and full of sin I am, Thou art full of truth and grace.
Spring Thou up with - in my heart, Rise to all e - ter - ni - ty.

74

187. Jesus! the very Thought is Sweet.

Tr. by Rev. JOHN M. NEALE, D.D., 1851.　　　　ROBERT SCHUMANN (1810—1856), 1839, op. 23.

1. Je - sus!—the ve - ry thought is sweet; In that dear name all heart-joys meet; But
2. No word is sung more sweet than this: No name is heard more full of bliss: No
3. I seek for Je - sus in re - pose, When round my heart its chambers close: A-
4. We fol - low Je - sus now, and raise The voice of prayer, the hymn of praise, That

sweet - er than sweet hon - ey far The glimp-ses of His pres-ence are.
tho't brings sweet - er com - fort nigh, Than Je - sus, Son of God most high.
broad, and when I shut the door, I long for Je - sus ev - er - more.
He at last may make us meet With Him to gain the heavenly seat. A-men

138. Jesus! Lover of my Soul.

C. WESLEY.　　　　(MARTYN.)　　　　S. B. MARSH.

1. Je - sus! lov - er of my soul, Let me to Thy bo - som fly While the bil lows

D. S.—Safe in - to the

FINE.　　　　— D.S.

near me roll, While the tempest still is high; { Hide me, O my Sav-iour! hide,
{ Till the storm of life is past;

ha - ven guide; Oh, receive my soul at last!

75

*39. Oh, for a thousand Tongues to sing.

C. WESLEY.   (DEDHAM.)   WM. GARDINER.

1. Oh, for a thou - sand tongues to sing My dear Re - deem - er's praise! The glo - ries of my God and King, The tri - umphs of His grace. A-men.

2 My gracious Master and my God!
Assist me to proclaim,
To spread, through all the earth abroad,
The honors of Thy name.

3 Jesus—the name that calms my fears,
That bids my sorrows cease;
'Tis music to my ravished ears;
'Tis life, and health, and peace.

4 He breaks the power of canceled sin,
He sets the prisoner free;
His blood can make the foulest clean;
His blood availed for me.

5 Let us obey, we then shall know,
Shall feel our sins forgiven;
Anticipate our heaven below,
And own that love is heaven.

140. PRAYER FOR A RIGHT HEART.

1 Oh, for a heart to praise my God,
A heart from sin set free;
A heart that always feels Thy blood
So freely shed for me!

2 A heart resigned, submissive, meek,
My dear Redeemer's throne;
Where only Christ is heard to speak,
Where Jesus reigns alone!

3 Oh, for a lowly, contrite heart,
Believing, true, and clean!
Which neither life nor death can part
From Him that dwells within.

4 A heart in every thought renewed,
And filled with love divine;
Perfect, and right, and pure, and good;
An image, Lord! of Thine.

5 Thy nature, gracious Lord, impart
Come quickly from above;
Write Thy new name upon my heart,—
Thy new, best name of Love.
       Charles Wesley, 1744, ab.

141. CHRIST OUR LIGHT.

1 Oh Very God of Very God,
And Very Light of Light,
Whose feet this earth's dark valley trod
That so it might be bright;

2 O guide us till our path is done,
And we have reached the shore
Where Thou, our Everlasting Sun,
Art shining evermore.

3 To wait in faith, and turn our face
To where the daylight springs,
Till Thou shalt come, our gloom to chase
With healing on Thy Wings.

4 To God the Father power and might
Both now and ever be;
To Him That is the Light of Light
And, Holy Ghost, to Thee!
       Rev. John M. Neale.

142. Oh, for a Closer walk with God.

WM. COWPER.   (BALERMA.)   HUGH WILSON.

1. Oh, for a clos - er walk with God, A calm and heavenly frame,—
2. Re - turn, O ho - ly Dove, re - turn, Sweet mes - sen - ger of rest!
3. The dear - est i - dol I have known, What-e'er that i - dol be,
4. So shall my walk be close with God, Calm and se - rene my frame;

A light to shine up - on the road That leads me to the Lamb!
I hate the sins that made Thee mourn, And drove Thee from my breast.
Help me to tear it from Thy throne, And wor - ship on - ly Thee.
So pur - er light shall mark the road That leads me to the Lamb. *A - men.*

143. Father whate'er of Earthly bliss.

ANNE STEELE.   (NAOMI.)   Fr. NÄGELI, by LOWELL MASON, 1836.

1. Father! whate'er of earthly bliss Thy sovereign will de - nies, Ac - cepted at Thy

throne of grace, Let this petition rise:— *Amen.*

2 "Give me a calm, a thankful heart,
From every murmur free;
The blessings of Thy grace impart,
And make me live to Thee.

3 "Let the sweet hope that Thou art mine:
My life and death attend;
Thy presence through my journey shine,
And crown my journey's end."

144. I Think, when I Read that Sweet Story.

DAVENANT.

Andantino.

1. I think, when I read that sweet sto - ry of old, When Je-sus was here a-mong
2. Yet still to His footstool in prayer I may go, And ask for a share in His
3. But thousands and thousands, who wander and fall, Nev - er heard of that heavenly

men, How He call'd lit - tle chil - dren, as lambs to His fold, I should
love; And if I now earn - est - ly seek Him be - low, I shall
home,—I should like them to know there is room for them all, And that

like to have been with them then. I wish that His hands had been
see Him and hear Him a - bove. In that beau - ti - ful place He has
Je - sus has bid them to come. I long for the joy of that

placed on my head, That His arm had been thrown a-round me, And that
gone to pre - pare For all that are washed and for - given; And
glo - ri - ous time, The sweet - est, and bright-est, and best; When the

I Think, when I Read.—Concluded.

I might have seen His kind look when He said, "Let the lit - tle ones come un-to me."
ma - ny dear children are gath - er - ing there, "For of such is the kingdom of heaven."
dear lit - tle children of ev - e - ry clime, Shall crowd to His arms and be blest.

145.   **I Think, when I Read.**

Mrs. JEMIMA LUKE.   English.

1. I think, when I read that sweet story of old, When Je - sus was here a-mong'men,
2. I wish that His hands had been placed on my head, That His arms had been thrown around me,

How He called little children as lambs to His fold, I should like to have been with them then.
And that I might have seen His kind looks when He said, "Let the little ones come unto me."

3 Yet still to His footstool in prayer I may go,
   And ask for a share in His love;
   And if I now earnestly seek Him below,
   I shall see Him and hear Him above:—

4 In that beautiful place He is gone to prepare
   For all who are washed and forgiven:
   And many dear children are gathering there,
   "For of such is the kingdom of heaven."

146.

1 O Thou, in whose presence my soul takes de-
   light,
   On whom in affliction I call,
   My comfort by day, and my song in the night,
   My hope, my salvation, my all !

2 Where dost Thou, dear Shepherd, resort with
   Thy sheep,
   To feed them in pastures of love?
   Say, why in the valley of death should I weep,
   Or alone in the wilderness rove?

3 O why should I wander an alien from Thee,
   Or cry in the desert for bread?
   Thy foes will rejoice when my sorrows they
   see,
   And smile at the tears I have shed.

4 Dear Shepherd, I hear, and will follow Thy
   call;
   I know the sweet sound of Thy voice;
   Restore and defend me, for Thou art my all.
   And in Thee I will ever rejoice.

147. The Morning Light is Breaking.

Rev. S. F. Smith.   (WEBB.)   George J. Webb, 1830.

1. The morning light is breaking, The darkness disappears! The sons of earth are waking

D. S. *Of na-tions in com-mo-tion,*

Fine. D.S.

To pen - i - ten-tial tears; Each breeze that sweeps the ocean Brings tidings from a - far,

Prepared for Zi-on's war.

2 See heathen nations bending
  Before the God we love,
  And thousand hearts ascending
  In gratitude above;
  While sinners, now confessing,
  The gospel call obey,
  And seek the Saviour's blessing—
  A nation in a day.

3 Blest river of salvation!
  Pursue thine onward way;
  Flow Thou to every nation,
  Nor in thy richness stay:
  Stay not till all the lowly
  Triumphant reach their home:
  Stay not till all the holy
  Proclaim—"The Lord is come!"

148.

1 Stand up!—stand up for Jesus!
  Ye soldiers of the cross;
  Lift high His royal banner,
  It must not suffer loss:
  From victory unto victory
  His army shall He lead,
  Till every foe is vanquished,
  And Christ is Lord indeed.

2 Stand up!—stand up for Jesus!
  The trumpet call obey;
  Forth to the mighty conflict,
  In this His glorious day;
  "Ye that are men, now serve Him,"
  Against unnumbered foes;
  Let courage rise with danger,
  And strength to strength oppose.

3 Stand up!—stand up for Jesus!
  Stand in His strength alone;
  The arm of flesh will fail you—
  Ye dare not trust your own:
  Put on the gospel armor,
  And, watching unto prayer,
  Where duty calls, or danger,
  Be never wanting there.

4 Stand up!—stand up for Jesus!
  The strife will not be long;
  This day, the noise of battle,
  The next, the victor's song:
  To him that overcometh,
  A crown of life shall be;
  He with the King of glory
  Shall reign eternally!

Rev. Geo. Duffield

80

149. The Ninety and Nine.

ELIZABETH C. CLEPHANE, 1868.   IRA D. SANKEY, by per.

1. There were ninety and nine that safe - ly lay In the shel - ter of the fold,
2. "Lord Thou hast here Thy ninety and nine; Are they not e - nough for Thee?"
3. But.... none of the ransomed ev - er knew How deep were the waters crossed;

But one was out on the hills a - way, Far off from the gates of gold—
But the Shepherd made an - swer: "This of mine Has wan - dered a - way from me;
Nor how dark was the night that the Lord pass'd thro', Ere He found His sheep that was lost;

A - way on the mountains wild and bare, A - way from the ten-der Shepherd's care,
And although the road be rough and steep, I go to the desert to find my sheep,
Out in the des-ert He heard its cry—'Twas helpless and sick, and ready to die,

A - way from the tender Shepherd's care.
I go to the desert to find my sheep."
'Twas helpless and sick, and ready to die.

4 And all through the mountains, thunder-riven,
    And up from the rocky steep,
There rose a cry to the gate of heaven,
    "Rejoice I have found my sheep!"
And the angels echoed around the throne,
    "Rejoice, for the Lord brings back His own,
Rejoice, for the Lord brings back His own."

150. Pass Me Not.

FANNY J. CROSBY, 1868. W. H. DOANE, by per.

1. Pass me not, O gen-tle Sav-iour, Hear my humble cry; While on
2. Let me at a throne of mer-cy Find a sweet re-lief; Kneel-ing
3. Trust-ing on-ly in Thy mer-it, Would I seek Thy face; Heal my
4. Thou the spring of all my com-fort, More than life for me; Whom have

CHORUS.

oth-ers Thou are call-ing, Do not pass me by. Sav-iour, Sav-iour, Hear my humble
there in deep con-tri-tion, Help my un-be-lief.
wounded, broken spir-it, Save me by Thy grace.
I on earth be-side Thee? Whom in heav'n but Thee.

cry, While on oth-ers Thou art call-ing, Do not pass me by.

151. Something for Jesus.

Rev. S. D. PHELPS, 1862. Rev. ROBERT LOWRY, by per.

1. Saviour! Thy dy-ing love Thou gavest me, Nor should I aught withhold, Dear Lord, from Thee;
2. At the blest mer-cy-seat, Pleading for me, My fee-ble faith looks up, Je-sus, to Thee;
3. Give me a faithful heart Likeness to Thee—That each de-part-ing day, Henceforth may see,

Something for Jesus.--Concluded.

In love my soul would bow, My heart fulfill its vow, Some offering bring Thee now, Something for Thee.
Help me the cross to bear, Thy wondrous love declare, Some song to raise, or pray'r, Something for Thee.
Some work of love begun, Some deed of kindness done, Some wand'rer sought and won, Something for Thee.

152. Abide with Me.

Rev. HENRY FRANCIS LYTE, 1847.

WILLIAM HENRY MONK, 1861.

1. A-bide with me; fast falls the e-ven-tide: The darkness deepens; Lord! with me abide;
2. I need Thy presence every passing hour; What, but Thy grace, can foil the tempter's pow'r?
3. Hold Thou Thy cross before my closing eyes; Shine thro the gloom, and point me to the skies;

When oth-er help-ers fail, and comforts flee, Help of the helpless! Oh! a-bide with me.
Who, like Thy-self, my guide and stay can be? Thro' cloud and sunshine, Oh! abide with me.
Heaven's morning breaks, and earth's vain shadows flee; In life and death, O Lord! abide with me.

153. CLOSING HYMN.

1 Saviour, again to Thy dear Name we raise
With one accord our parting hymn of praise;
We stand to bless Thee ere our worship cease,
Then, lowly kneeling, wait Thy word of peace.

2 Grant us Thy peace upon our homeward way;
With Thee began, with Thee shall end the day;
Guard Thou the lips from sin, the hearts from shame,
That in this house have called upon Thy Name.

3 Grant us Thy peace, Lord, thro' the coming night,
Turn Thou for us its darkness into light;
From harm and danger keep Thy children free,
For dark and light are both alike to Thee.

4 Grant us Thy peace throughout our early life,
Our balm in sorrow, and our stay in strife;
Then, when Thy voice shall bid our conflict cease,
Call us, O Lord, to Thine eternal peace.

154. Oh, Jesus, Thou art Standing.

W. W. How, 1854.   (FOREST HYMN.)   MENDELSSOHN.

cres.   *f*

1. Oh Je - sus, Thou art standing Out-side the fast closed door, In low - ly patience
2. Oh Je - sus, Thou art pleading In accents meek and low, — "I died for you my

dim.   Oh, love that passeth knowl - edge,

wait - ing To pass the threshold o'er: Oh, love that pass - eth knowl - edge.
chil - dren, And will ye treat me so?" O Lord with shame and sor - row

f   *p*

So pa - tiently to wait! Oh, sin that hath no e - qual, So fast to bar the
We o - pen now the door: Dear Saviour, en - ter, en - ter, And leave us nev - er-

f   So pa - tient - ly to wait,
    dim.

gate! Oh, love that pass - eth knowledge, So pa - - - tiently to wait!
more! O Lord, with shame and sor - row We o - - - pen now the door:

84

155. Hark, what mean those Holy Voices.

JOHN CAWOOD.   (VESPER HYMN.)   D. BORTNIANSKY.

1. Hark! what mean those holy voic-es, Sweet-ly warb-ling thro' the skies? Sure th'angel - ic
2. "Peace on earth, good-will from heaven Reaching far as man is found; Souls redeem'd and
3. Let us learn the wondrous sto - ry Of our great Re-deemer's birth; Spread the brightness

host re - joic - es; Loudest hal - le - lu - jahs rise. List-en to the wondrous sto - ry,
sins for - giv - en; Loud our golden harps shall sound." List-en to the wondrous sto - ry,
of His glo - ry Till it cov - er all the earth, List-en to the wondrous sto - ry,

Which they chant in hymns of joy, "Glo - ry in the high - est, glo - ry! Glo-ry be to

God most high!" Ju - bi - la - te, Ju - bi - la - te, Ju - bi - la - te, A - men.

87

156. One Sweetly Solemn Thought.

Miss PHOEBE CAREY.   PHILIP PHILLIPS, by per.

1. One sweet - ly sol - emn thought Comes to me o'er and o er, I'm
2. Near - er my Fa - ther's house, Where ma - ny mansions be; Near-
3. Near - er the bound of life, Where bur - dens are laid down; Near-
4. But, ly - ing dark be - tween, Wind - ing down thro' the night, There

near - er home to - day, to - day, Than I have been be - fore.
er to - day the great white throne, Near - er the crys - tal sea.
er to leave the heav - y cross; Near - er to gain the crown.
rolls the deep and un - known stream That leads at last to light.

CHORUS.

Near - er my home, Near - er my home, Near - er my home to

day, to - day, Than I have been be - fore.

5 Ev'n now, perchance, my feet
 Are slipping on the brink,
And I, to-day, am nearer home,—
 Nearer than now I think.

6 Father, perfect my trust !
 Strengthen my power of faith !
Nor let me stand, at last, alone
 Upon the shore of death.

88

157. Blest be the Tie that Binds.

J. FAWCETT.   (BOYLSTON.)   LOWELL MASON,

1. Blest be the tie that binds Our hearts in Chris-tian love: The fel-low-ship of
2. Be - fore our Fa-ther's throne We pour our ar - dent prayers; Our fears, our hopes, our
3. We share our mutual woes, Our mu-tual bur-dens bear; And oft - en for each
4. When we a - sun-der part, It gives us in - ward pain; But we shall still be

kindred minds Is like to that a - bove.
aims are one, Our comforts and our cares.
oth - er flows The sympathiz - ing tear.
joined in heart, And hope to meet a - gain.

5 This glorious hope revives
   Our courage by the way;
While each in expectation lives,
   And longs to see the day.

6 From sorrow, toil and pain,
   And sin we shall be free,
And perfect love and friendship reign
   Through all eternity.

158. One Sweetly Solemn Thought.

(DUNBAR.)   E. W. DUNBAR.

1. One sweet - ly sol - emn thought Comes to me o'er and o'er, —

CHO. — There'll be no sor - row there, There'll be no sor - row there;

D. C.

Near - er my home to - day am I Than e'er I've been be - fore.

In heaven a - bove, where all is love, There'll be no sor - row there.

87

159. Wonderful Words of Life.

P. P. Bliss.

P. P. Bliss, by per.

1. Sing them o - ver a - gain to me, Won - der - ful words of Life,
2. Christ, the bless - ed One gives to all Won - der - ful words of Life,
3. Sweet - ly ech - o the gos - pel call, Won - der - ful words of Life,

Let me more of their beau - ty see, Wonder - ful words of Life. Words of life and
Siu - ner, list to the lov - ing call, Wonder - ful words of Life. All so free - ly
Of - fer par - don and peace to all, Wonder - ful words of Life. Je - sus, on - ly

beau - ty, Teach me faith and du - ty; Beau - ti - ful words, won - der - ful words,
giv - en, Woo - ing us to hea - ven.
Sav - iour, Sanc - ti - fy for - ev - er.

Wonder-ful words of Life, Beau-ti-ful words, wonderful words, Wonderful words of Life.

Copyright by J. Church & Co

88

160.   It came upon the Midnight clear.

Rev. E. H. Sears, 1850.   (CAROL.)   R. Storrs Willis, 1860., alt.

Joyful.

1. It came up - on the midnight clear, That glorious song of old, From angels bending near the earth, To touch their harps of gold: "Peace on the earth, good-will to men From heaven's all gracious King;" The world in solemn stillness lay To hear the angels sing. A - men.

2 Still through the cloven skies they come,
　With peaceful wings unfurl'd;
And still their heavenly music floats
　O'er all the weary world:
Above its sad and lowly plai 1s
　They bend on hovering wing,
And ever o'er its Babel-sounds
　The blessed angels sing,

3 O ye beneath life's crushing load,
　Whose forms are bending low,
Who toil along the climbing way,
　With painful steps and slow !

Look now, for glad and golden hours
　Come swiftly on the wing;
O rest beside the weary road,
　And hear the angels sing.

4 For lo, the days are hastening on,
　By prophets seen of old,
When with the ever-circling years
　Shall come the time foretold,
When the new heaven and earth shall own
　The Prince of Peace their King,
And the whole world send back the song
　Which now the angels sing.

161.
Day by Day the Manna fell.
(MERCY.)

Arr. from Louis M. Gottschalk.

1. Day by day the man - na fell; Oh, to learn this les - son well!
2. "Day by day," the prom - ise reads, Dai - ly strength for dai - ly needs;

Still by con-stant mer - cy fed, Give us, Lord, our dai - ly bread.
Cast fore - bod - ing fears a - way, Take the man - na of to - day.

3 Lord, our times are in Thy hand;
All our sanguine hopes have plann'd
To Thy wisdom we resign,
And would mould our wills to Thine.

4 Thou our daily task shalt give;
Day by day to Thee we live;
So shall added years fulfil
Not our own, our Father's will.

162.

1 Holy Ghost! with light divine,
Shine upon this heart of mine;
Chase the shades of night away,
Turn my darkness into day.

2 Holy Ghost! with power divine,
Cleanse this guilty heart of mine;
Long hath sin, without control,
Held dominion o'er my soul.

3 Holy Ghost! with joy divine,
Cheer this saddened heart of mine;
Bid my many woes depart,
Heal my wounded, bleeding heart.

4 Holy Spirit! all-divine,
Dwell within this heart of mine;
Cast down every idol-throne,
Reign supreme—and reign alone.

A. Reed.

163.

1 Gracious Spirit, Love divine!
Let Thy light within me shine;
All my guilty fears remove,
Fill me with Thy heavenly love.

2 Speak Thy pardoning grace to me,
Set the burdened sinner free;
Lead me to the Lamb of God;
Wash me in His precious blood.

3 Life and peace to me impart,
Seal salvation on my heart;
Breathe Thyself into my breast,—
Earnest of immortal-rest.

4 Let me never from Thee stray,
Keep me in the narrow way;
Fill my soul with joy divine,
Keep me, Lord, forever Thine.

John Stocker.

164. Softly now the Light of Day.

GEO. W. DOANE, D.D.   (HOLLEY.)   GEO. HEWS 1834.

1. Soft - ly now the light of day Fades up - on my sight a - way;
2. Thou, whose all - per - vad - ing eye Naught es - capes with - out; with - in,

Free from care, from la - bor free, Lord, I would commune with Thee.
Par - don each in - firm - i - ty, O - pen fault, and se - cret sin. *Amen.*

3 Soon, for me, the light of day
Shall for ever pass away;
Then, from sin and sorrow free,
Take me, Lord, to dwell with Thee.

4 Thou who, sinless, yet hast known
All of man's infirmity;
Then from Thine eternal throne,
Jesus, look with pitying eye.

165. THE COMFORTER.

1 HOLY Spirit, Blessed Dove,
Sent by Jesus from above,
Sent to be our Friend most dear,
And a Comforter to cheer.

2 Gentle Guide and Helper sweet,
Lead our weary, wayworn feet
Safely through this world of care,
Till they reach Thy dwelling fair.

3 Tender Friend, Companion blest,
Deign to be our constant Guest,
All that grieves Thee put away,
And with us for ever stay.

4 Form in us each good desire,
Quicken them with holy fire,
Till the life on love's strong wing
Upward soar, and soaring sing.

5 Holy Spirit, Blessed Dove,
Comforter, Whose Name is Love,
Helper, Friend, Companion, Guide,
Evermore with us abide.

166. A CALL TO PRAYER.

1 COME, my soul, thy suit prepare,
Jesus loves to answer prayer;
He Himself has bid thee pray,
Therefore will not say thee nay.

2 With my burden I begin:—
Lord! remove this load of sin;
Let Thy blood. for sinners spilt,
Set my conscience free from guilt.

3 Lord! I come to Thee for rest;
Take possession of my breast:
There, Thy blood-bought right maintain,
And, without a rival, reign.

4 While I am a pilgrim here,
Let Thy love my spirit cheer;
As my Guide, my Guard, my Friend,
Lead me to my journey's end.

5 Show me what I have to do,
Every hour my strength renew;
Let me live a life of faith,
Let me die Thy people's death.

J. Newton.

167. Hiding in Thee.

Rev. WILLIAM O. CUSHING.

IRA D. SANKEY, by per.

1. O.... safe to the Rock that is high - er than I, My.. soul in its
2. In the calm of the noon-tide, in sor - row's lone hour, In.. times when temp-
3. How oft in the con - flict, when press'd by the foe, I have fled to my

con - flicts and sor - rows would fly; So.... sin - ful, so wea - ry, Thine,
ta - tion casts o'er me its power; In the tem - pests of life, on its
Ref - uge and breathed out my woe; How oft - en when tri - als like

Thine would I be; Thou blest "Rock of A - ges," I'm hid - ing in Thee.
wide, heav-ing sea, Thou blest "Rock of A - ges," I'm hid - ing in Thee.
sea - bil - lows roll, Have I hid - den in Thee, O Thou Rock of my soul.

REFRAIN.

Hid-ing in Thee, Hid-ing in Thee, Thou blest "Rock of A - ges," I'm hid - ing in Thee.

168. The Prince of Peace.

L. ERHARDT, by per.

In march time.

1. To hail Thy ris - ing Sun of life, The gath'ring nations come, Joyous as when the
2. For Thou our bur-den hast removed, Th'oppressor's reign is broke; Thy fie - ry conflict
3. "To us the promised Child is born, To us the Son is given; Him shall the tribes of
4. His pow'r in-creas-ing still shall spread, His reign no end shall know; Justice shall guard His

CHORUS.

reap - ers bear Their harvest treas-ures home. His Name shall be, His
with the foe Has burst his cru - el yoke.
earth o - bey, And all the hosts of heaven."
throne a - bove, And peace abound be - low. His Name shall be,

Name shall be the Prince of Peace, His Name shall be the Prince of Peace For ev - er-more a -

The Prince of Peace, the Prince, the

The Prince of Peace, the Prince of

dored, The Won-der - ful, the Coun-sel - lor, The mighty God and Lord.

Prince of Peace, Prince, the Prince, the Prince, the Prince of Peace.

Peace, the Prince of Peace, the Prince of Peace.

93

169. Awake, my Soul, to Joyful Lays.

S. MEDLEY. (LOVING KINDNESS.) Western Melody.

1. A - wake, my soul, to joyful lays, And sing thy great Redeemer's praise; He justly claims a
2. He saw me ruined in the fall, Yet loved me, notwithstanding all; He saved me from my

song from me, His lov-ing-kindness, oh, how free! Loving-kindness, loving-kindness,
lost es - tate: His lov-ing-kindness, oh, how great! Loving-kindness, loving-kindness,

His lov-ing-kindness, oh, how free!
His lov-ing-kindness, oh, how great! A-men.

3 Though numerous hosts of mighty foes,
  Though earth and hell my way oppose,
  He safely leads my soul along:
  His loving-kindness, oh, how strong!

4 When trouble, like a gloomy cloud,
  Has gathered thick and thundered loud,
  He near my soul has always stood:
  His loving-kindness, oh, how good!

170. Come, Jesus, Redeemer.

RAY PALMER, D. D. (CAPERNAUM.) MOZART, arr. by Rev. G. G. PHIPPS.

1. Come, Je-sus, Re-deem - er, abide Thou with me, Come gladden my spirit that waiteth for Thee,
2. Without Thee but weakness, with Thee I am strong; By day Thou shalt lead me, by night be my song:
3. Thy love, O how faithful, so tender, so pure! Thy promise, faith's anchor, how stedfast and sure!
4. Breathe, breathe ou my spirit, oft ruffled, Thy peace; From restless, vain wishes, bid Thou my heart cease,

Come, Jesus, Redeemer.—Concluded.

Thy smile ev'ry shadow shall chase from my heart, And soothe ev'ry sorrow though keen be its smart.
Though dangers surround me, I still every fear, Since Thou, the Most Mighty, my Helper, art near.
That love, like sweet sunshine, my cold heart can warm, That promise make steady my soul in the storm.
In Thee all its longings henceforward shall end, Till glad to Thy presence my soul shall ascend.

171. Awake, my Soul, stretch every Nerve.

P. DODDRIDGE.   (CHRISTMAS.)   GEO. F. HANDEL.

1. A - wake, my soul, stretch ev - ery nerve, And press with vig - or   on;   A heavenly
2. A   cloud of wit - ness - es   a - round Hold Thee in full   sur - vey;   For-get the

race demands thy zeal, And an   immor-tal crown,   And an im - mor-tal crown.
steps al-read - y   trod, And onward urge thy way,   And on-ward urge thy way,   A-men.

3 'Tis God's all-animating voice,
   That calls thee from on high,
 'Tis His own hand presents the prize
   To thine aspiring eye.

4 Blest Saviour, introduced by Thee
   Have I my race begun;
 And, crowned with victory, at Thy feet
   I'll lay my honors down.

172.   CHRISTMAS.

1 While shepherds watched their flocks by night,
   All seated on the ground,
 The angel of the Lord came down,
   And glory shone around.

2 "Fear not," said he,—for mighty dread
   Had seized their troubled mind,—
 "Glad tidings of great joy I bring,
   To you and all mankind.

3 "To you, in David's town, this day
   Is born, of David's line,
 The Saviour, who is Christ the Lord;
   And this shall be the sign:

4 "The heavenly babe you there shall find.
   To human view displayed,
 All meanly wrapped in swathing-bands,
   And in a manger laid."

5 Thus spake the seraph; and forthwith
   Appeared a shining throng
 Of angels, praising God on high,
   Who thus addressed their song:

6 "All glory be to God on high,
   And to the earth be peace:
 Good-will henceforth from heaven to men,
   Begin and never cease."

Tate and Brady.

95

173. Sing of the wonders of His Love.

DOROTHY ANN THRUPP. (ALL HALLOWS.) English.

Joyous.

1. Come, Chris - tian children, come and raise Your voice with one ac - cord;
2. Sing of the wonders of His Truth, And read in ev - ery page
3. Sing of the wonders of His Grace, Who made and keeps you His,

FINE.

Come, sing in joy - ful songs of praise The glo - ries of your Lord.
The prom - ise made to ear - liest youth Fulfilled to lat - est age.
And guides you to th' ap-pointed place At His right hand in bliss.

Sing of the won - ders of His love, And loud - est prais - es give,
Sing of the won - ders of His power, Who with His own right arm
Sing of the won - ders of His Name, And Je - sus Christ a - dore;

D. C.

To Him who left His throne a - bove, And died that you might live.
Up - holds and keeps you hour by hour, And shields from ev - ery harm.
Him for your Lord and God proclaim, And praise Him ev - er - more. A - men.

*After Fine,
last verse.*

174. The Light of the World is Jesus.

P. P. BLISS. P. P. BLISS, by per.

1. The whole world was lost in the darkness of sin; The Light of the world is Je-sus,
2. No darkness have we who in Je-sus a-bide, The Light of the world is Je-sus;
3. Ye dwellers in darkness with sin-blind-ed eyes, The Light of the world is Je-sus;
4. No need of the sunlight in heaven, we're told, The Light of the world is Je-sus;

Like sunshine at noon-day His glo-ry shone in, The Light of the world is Je-sus.
We walk in the Light when we fol-low our Guide, The Light of the world is Je-sus.
Go, wash, at His bid-ding, and light will a-rise, The Light of the world is Je-sus.
The Lamb is the light in the Cit-y of Gold, The Light of the world is Je-sus.

CHORUS.

Come to the Light, 'tis shin-ing for thee; Sweetly the Light has dawn'd up-on me,

Once I was blind, but now I can see; The Light of the world is Je-sus.

175.　　　Glory to God in the Highest.

Old English.　　　　　　　　　　　　　　　　　　ARTHUR H. BROWN.

1. When Christ was born of Ma - ry free, In Beth - le - hem that fair cit - ie,
2. Herds-men be - held these An - gels bright, To them ap-pear - ing with great light,

An - gels sang there with mirth and glee, "In ex - cel - sis glo - ri - a."
Who said, God's Son is born to - night, "In ex - cel - sis glo - ri - a."

CHORUS.

In ex - cel - sis glo - ri - a, In ex - cel - sis glo - ri - a,

In ex - cel - sis glo - ri - a, In ex - cel - sis glo - ri - a.

3 The King is come to save mankind,
As in the Scripture truths we find,
Therefore this song we have in mind,
  "In excelsis gloria."

4 Then, dear Lord, for Thy great grace
Grant us in bliss to see Thy face,
That we may sing to Thy solace,
  "In excelsis gloria."

176.   **Who are these in bright array.**

J. MONTGCMERY.   (BEULAH.)   Arr. by ELAM IVES.

1. Who are these in bright ar - ray, This in - nu - mer - a - ble throng Round the al - tar,
2. These thro' fi - ery tri - als trod; These from great af-flictions came: Now be - fore the

night and day Hymning one triumph-ant song?—"Worthy is the Lamb, once slaiu, Blessing,
throne of God, Sealed with His al - migh-ty name, Clad in raiment pure and white, Vic - tor-

hon - or, glo - ry, power, Wisdom, riches, to ob - tain, New do - min-ion every hour."
palms in ev - ery hand, Through their Redeemer's might, More than conquerors they stand.

3 Hunger, thirst, disease unknown,
    On immortal fruits they feed;
Them the Lamb, amid the throne,
    Shall to living fountains lead:
Joy and gladness banish sighs—
Perfect love dispel all fears—
And for ever from their eyes
God shall wipe away the tears.

177.

1 PALMS of glory, raiment bright,
    Crowns that never fade away,
Gird and deck the saints in light;
    Priests, and kings, and conquerors, they.
Yet the conquerors bring their palms
    To the Lamb amid the throne;
And proclaim, in joyful psalms,
    Victory through His cross alone.

2 Kings for harps their crowns resign,
    Crying, as they strike the chords—
"Take the kingdom; it is thine,
    King of kings, and Lord of lords."
Round the altar, priests confess,
    If their robes are white as snow,
'Twas their Saviour's righteousness,
    And His blood that made them so.

3 Who are these? On earth they dwelt,
    Sinners once of Adam's race;
Guilt, and fear, and suffering felt,
    But were saved by sovereign grace.
They were mortal, too, like us:
    Ah, when we, like them shall die,
May our souls, translated thus,
    Triumph, reign, and shine, on high !

James Montgomery.

178. Mary to her Saviour's Tomb.

Rev. JOHN NEWTON   (MARTYN.)   SIMEON B. MARSH, 1834.

1. Ma - ry to her Sav-iour's tomb Hast-ed at the ear-ly dawn;
2. Je - sus, who is al - ways near, Though too oft - en un - per - ceived,

Spice she brought and sweet per-fume; But the Lord she loved was gone.
Came, His droop - ing child to cheer, Kind - ly ask - ing why she grieved.

For a-while she weep-ing stood, Struck with sor - row and sur - prise,
Though at first she knew Him not, When He called her by her name,

Shed - ding tears a plen-teous flood, For her heart supplied her eyes.
Then her griefs were all for - got, For she found He was the same.

3 Grief and sighing quickly fled
  When she heard His welcome voice;
Just before, she thought Him dead,
  Now, He bids her heart rejoice.
What a change His word can make,
  Turning darkness into day!
You who weep for Jesus' sake,
  He will wipe your tears away.

4 He who came to comfort ner,
  When she thought her all was lost,
Will for your relief appear,
  Though you now are tempest-tost.
On His word your burden cast,
  On His love your thoughts employ;
Weeping for a while may last,
  But the morning brings the joy.

179. My life Flows on in Endless Song.

ANON.
Rev. R. LOWRY.

1. My life flows on in end-less song; A-bove Earth's la-men-ta-tion, I catch the sweet, tho'
2. What tho' my joys and comfort die? The Lord my Saviour liv-eth; What tho' the darkness
3. I lift my eyes; the cloud grows thin; I see the blue a - bove it; And day by day this

far - off hymn That hails a new cre - a - tion; Through all the tu - mult and the strife, I
gather round? Songs in the night He giv-eth, No storm can shake my in-most calm, While
pathway smooths, Since first I learned to love it; The peace of Christ makes fresh my heart, A

hear the mu - sic ringing; It finds an ech - o in my soul— How can I keep from singing?
to that refuge clinging; Since Christ is the Lord of heaven and earth, How can I keep from singing?
fountain ev - er springing; All things are mine since I am His— How can I keep from singing?

180. CONVERSE WITH GOD.
Tune—MARTYN.

1 PLEASANT are Thy courts above,
In the land of light and love;
Pleasant are Thy courts below
In this land of sin and woe.
Oh, my spirit longs and faints,
For the converse of Thy saints,
For the brightness of Thy face,
King of glory, God of grace.

2 Happy souls, their praises flow
Even in this vale of woe;
Waters in the desert rise,
Manna feeds them from the skies:

On they go from strength to strength;
Till they reach Thy throne at length;
At Thy feet adoring fall,
Who hast led them safe through all.

3 Lord be mine this prize to win;
Guide me through a world of sin;
Keep me by Thy saving grace;
Give me at Thy side a place.
Sun and Shield alike Thou art;
Guide and guard my erring heart;
Grace and glory flow from Thee,
Shower, O shower them, Lord, on me.

Rev. Henry Francis Lyte, 1884.

181. Art thou weary, Art thou languid?

Tr. by J. M. NEALE   (STEPHANOS.)   Sir H. W. BAKER. 1868.

1. Art thou wea - ry, art thou lan - guid, Art thou sore distressed?
2. Hath He marks to lead me to Him, If He be my Guide?
3. Is there di - a - dem, as Mon - arch, That His brow a - dorns?

"Come to me," saith One, "and com - ing. Be at rest!"
"In His feet and hands are wound - prints, And His side."
"Yea, a crown, in ver - y . sure - ty; But of thorns." A-men.

4 If I find Him, if I follow,
  What His guerdon here?—
"Many a sorrow, many a labor,
  Many a tear."

5 If I still hold closely to Him,
  What hath He at last?—
"Sorrow vanquished, labor ended,
  Jordan passed."

6 If I ask Him to receive me,
  Will He say me nay?—
"Not till earth, and not till heaven
  Pass away."

7 Finding, following, keeping, struggling,
  Is He sure to bless?—
"Saints, apostles, prophets, martyrs,
  Answer, Yes."

* Can be sung responsively—One part of the school singing the question in the first two lines, and the answer be given by the other part, or by the whole school.

182. Come, let us Join our Cheerful Songs.

I. WATTS.   (ST. MARTINS.)   WM. TANSUR.

1. Come, let us join our cheer - ful songs With an - gels round the throne;
2. "Wor - thy the Lamb that died," they cry, "To be ex - alt - ed thus!"
3. Je - sus is wor - thy to re - ceive Hon - or and power di - vine;

Come, let us Join.—Concluded.

Ten thousand thou - sand are their tongues, But all their joys are one.
"Wor - thy the Lamb!" our lips re - ply, "For He was slain for us."
And bless-ings, more than ' we can give, Be, Lord, for ev - er Thine! *Amen.*

4 Let all that dwell above the sky,
  And air, and earth, and seas,
  Conspire to lift Thy glories high,
  And speak Thine endless praise.

5 The whole creation join in one,
  To bless the sacred name,
  Of Him who sits upon the throne,
  And to adore the Lamb!

183.   We are on our Journey home.

Rev CH. BEECHER, 1855.   (MT. BLANC.)   J. J. HUSBAND, 1796.

1. We are on our journey home, Where Christ our Lord is gone; We shall meet around His throne,

When He makes His people one In the new, in the new. In the new Je-ru-sa-lem. *Amen.*

2 We can see that distant home,
  Though clouds rise dark between;
  Faith views the radiant dome,
  And a lustre flashes keen,
  From the new Jerusalem.

3 O glory shining far
  From the never-setting sun!
  O trembling morning star!
  Our journey's almost done
  To the new Jerusalem.

4 O holy, heavenly home!
  O, rest eternal there!
  When shall the exiles come,
  Where they cease from earthly care.
  In the new Jerusalem.

5 Our hearts are breaking now,
  Those mansions fair to see;
  O Lord! Thy heavens bow,
  And raise us up with Thee
  To the new Jerusalem.

184. The Cross of Jesus.

Miss E. C. CLEPHANE.   IRA D. SANKEY, by per.

1. Be - neath the cross of Je - sus I fain would take my stand— The
2. O safe and hap - py shel - ter, O ref - uge tried and sweet, O
3. Up - on that Cross of Je - sus, Mine eye at times can see The

shad - ow of a might - y Rock, With - in a wea - ry land, A
tryst - ing-place where Heav - en's love, And Heav - en's jus - tice meet! As
ver - y dy - ing form of One, Who suf - fered there for me And

home with - in the wil - der-ness, A rest up - on the way, From the
to the Ho - ly Pa - tri-arch That wondrous dream was given, So...
from my smit-ten heart with tears, Two won - ders I con - fess,— The....

burn - ing of the noon - tide heat, And the bur - den of the day.
seems my Saviour's Cross to me, A.... lad - der up to heaven.
won - ders of His glo - rious love, And....my own worth-less - ness.

185. How firm a Foundation, ye Saints of the Lord?

GEORGE KEITH.   (PORTUGUESE HYMN.)   MARCOS PORTUGAL, ab. 1796.

1. How firm a foun - da-tion, ye saints of the Lord! Is laid for your faith in His
2. "Fear not, I am with thee, oh, be not dis-mayed, For I am thy God, I will

ex - cel-lent word! What more can He say, than to you He hath said, To you, who for
still give thee aid; I'll strengthen thee, help thee, and cause thee to stand, Up-held by my

ref-uge to Je- sus hath fled, To you, who for ref-uge to Je - sus have fled?
gracious, om - ni-potent hand, Up - held by my gracious, om - ni- po-tent hand. A-men.

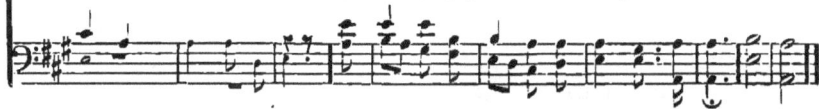

3 "When through the deep waters I call thee to
    go,
The rivers of sorrow shall not overflow;
For I will be with thee thy trouble to bless,
And sanctify to thee thy deepest distress.

4 "When through fiery trials thy pathway shall
    lie,
My grace, all-sufficient, shall be thy supply;
The flame shall not hurt thee; I only design
Thy dross to consume, and thy gold to refine.

5 "Ev'n down to old age all my people shall prove
My sovereign, eternal, unchangeable love;
And then, when gray hairs shall their temples
    adorn,
Like lambs they shall still in my bosom be borne.

6 "The soul that on Jesus hath leaned for repose,
I will not—I will not desert to his foes;
That soul—though all hell should endeavor to
    shake,
I'll never—no never —no never forsake!"

186. Carol, Sweetly Carol.

F. J. C.

THEO. E. PERKINS, 1867.

1. Ca - rol, sweetly ca - rol, A Saviour born to - day; Bear the joy-ful tidings. Oh,
2. Ca - rol, sweetly ca - rol, As when the An - gel throng O'er the vales of Ju-dah, A -
3. Ca - rol, sweetly ca - rol, The happy Christmas time; Hark I the bells are pealing Their

bear them far a - way, Ca - rol, sweetly ca - rol, Till earth's re-mot-est bound Shall
woke the heavenly song, Ca - rol, sweetly ca - rol, Good will, with peace and love,
mer - ry, mer - ry chime; Ca - rol, sweetly ca - rol, Ye shining ones a - bove,

CHORUS.

hear the mighty cho-rus, And ech - o back the sound. Ca - rol, sweetly ca - rol,
Glo - ry in the highest, To God who reigns a-bove.
Sing in loudest numbers, Oh, sing redeem-ing love.

Ca - rol,

Ca-rol sweetly,

Ca - rol, sweetly to - day; Bear the joy - ful tidings, Oh, bear them far a - way.
Ca - - rol, Ca-rol,

Ca - rol, sweetly to - day.

187. Once in Royal David's City.

Mrs. C. F. ALEXANDER. (IRBY.) HENRY J. GAUNTLETT.

Joyful.

1. Once in roy - al Da - vid's ci - ty Stood a low - ly cat - tle
2. He came down to earth from heav - en, Who is God and Lord of
3. And, through all His won - drous childhood, He would hon - or, and o -

shed, Where a moth - er laid her Ba - by, In a
all, And His shel - ter was a sta - ble, And His
bey, Love and watch the low - ly maid - en In whose

man - ger for His bed: Ma - ry was that moth - er mild, Je - sus
cra - dle was a stall; With the poor, the mean, and lowly, Lived on
gen - tle arms He lay; Chris-tian chil - dren all must be Mild, o -

Christ her lit - tle Child.
earth our Sav - iour Holy.
be - dient, good as He. *A-men.*

4 For He is our childhood's Pattern,
   Day by day like us He grew,
He was little, weak, and helpless,
   Tears and smiles, like us, He knew;
And He feeleth for our sadness,
And He shareth in our gladness.

5 And our eyes at last shall see Him;
   Through His own redeeming love,
For that Child so dear and gentle
   Is our Lord in heaven above;
And He leads His children on
To the place where He is gone.

188.

(Trans. by J. BORTHWICK.)

Von WEBER, 1820, arr. H. P. M.

1. My Je - sus as Thou wilt! Oh! may Thy will be mine; In - to Thy
2. My Je - sus as Thou wilt! All shall be well for me; Each changing

hand of love I would my all re - sign; Thro' sor - row, or thro' joy, Conduct me
fu - ture scene I glad - ly trust with Thee: Straight to my home a - bove I trav - el

as Thine own, And help me still to say, My Lord, Thy will be done!
calm - ly on, And sing, in life or death, My Lord, Thy will be done! A-men.

189. THY WAY, NOT MINE.

1 Thy way, not mine, O Lord,
However dark it be!
Lead me by Thine own hand;
Choose out the path for me.
I dare not choose my lot;
I would not, if I might:
Choose Thou for me, my God
So shall I walk aright.

2 The kingdom that I seek,
Is Thine; so let the way
That leads to it be Thine,
Else I must surely stray.

Take Thou my cup, and it
With joy or sorrow fill,
As best to Thee may seem;
Choose Thou my good and ill.

3 Choose Thou for me my friends,
My sickness or my health;
Choose Thou my cares for me,
My poverty or wealth.
Not mine, not mine the choice,
In things or great or small;
Be Thou my Guide, my Strength,
My Wisdom, and my All.

Rev. H. Bonar.

190.   Holy! Holy! Lord God Almighty!

Bp. Reginald Heber, 1827.   Rev. J. B. Dykes, 1861.

1. Ho - ly, Ho - ly, Ho - ly! Lord God al - might - y!
2. Ho - ly, Ho - ly, Ho - ly! all the saints a - dore Thee,
3. Ho - ly, Ho - ly, Ho - ly! tho' the dark - ness hide Thee,
4. Ho - ly, Ho - ly, Ho - ly! Lord God al - might - y!

Ear - ly in the morn - ing our song shall rise to Thee;
Cast - ing down their gold-en crowns a - round the glass - y sea;
Though the eye of sin-ful man Thy glo - ry may not see,
All Thy works shall praise thy Name, in earth, and sky, and sea;

Ho - ly, Ho - ly, Ho - ly! Mer - ci - ful and might - y!
Cher - u - bim and Ser - a - phim fall - ing down be - fore Thee,
On - ly Thou art Ho - ly, there is none be - side Thee
Ho - ly, Ho - ly, Ho - ly! Mer - ci - ful and might - y!

God in Three Per - sons, bless - ed Trin - i - ty!
Which wert, and art, and ev - er - more shalt be.
Per - fect in power, in love, and pu - ri - ty.
God in Three Per - sons, bless - ed Trin - i - ty! A - men.

191.   The Home Over There.

Rev. D. W. C. Huntington.   Tullius C. O'Kane, by per.

1. Oh, think of the home o - ver there, By the side of the riv - er of
2. Oh, think of the friends o - ver there, Who be - fore us the jour - ney have
3. My Sav - iour is now o - ver there, There my kin - dred and friends are at
4. I'll soon be at home o - ver there, For the end of my jour - ney I

light,   Where the saints, all im - mor - tal and fair, Are
trod,   Of the songs that they breathe on the air. In their
rest;   Then a - way from my sor - row and care, Let me
see;   Ma - ny dear to my heart, o - ver there, Are

REFRAIN.

robed in their garments of white, o - ver there; O - ver there,   o - ver
home in the pal - ace of God, o - ver there; O - ver there,   o - ver
fly to the land of the blest, o - ver there; O - ver there,   o - ver
watching and wait - ing for me, o - ver there; O - ver there,   o - ver

o - ver there,

there,   Oh, think of the home o - ver there, o - ver there; O - ver
there,   Oh, think of the friends o - ver there, o - ver there; O - ver
there,   My Sav - iour is now o - ver there, o - ver there; O - ver
there,   I'll soon be at home o - ver there, o - ver there; O - ver

o - ver there,   o - ver there.

110

The Home Over There.—Concluded.

there, o - ver there, o - ver there,   o - ver there, Oh, think of   the home o - ver there.
there, o - ver there, o - ver there,   o - ver there, Oh, think of   the friends o - ver there.
there, o - ver there, o - ver there,   o - ver there, My Sav-iour   is now   o - ver there.
there, o - ver there, o - ver there,   o - ver there, I'll soon be   at home   o - ver there.

o - ver there

192.

O Shepherd Crowned.

(A SONG CHANT.)

F. S. WILSON.   Theme—BEETHOVEN, arr. by G. G. PHIPPS, 1876.

1. O Shepherd, crowned with thorns, seek-ing Thy flock,   By cave and rock,
2. When clouds and storms hide up the sun - ny sky,   When night draws nigh,

Where through the desert briars from.....Life   they   fly,   And   run   to   die,
When winds sweep bleak and drear the ... des - ert   air,   Then   ev - er - more

No helper but Thyself is.............. left   us   now,   Help,   Thou, help, Thou!
To listen to our cries of.............. weak - ness, bow,   Help,   Thou, help, Thou!

111

193. Hark the Voice of Jesus Calling.

Daniel March, D. D.   (MISSION SONG.)   P. P. Van Arsdale.

1. Hark! the voice of Je - sus call-ing,— Who will go and work to - day?

Fields are white, the har - vest wait-ing, Who will bear the sheaves a - way?

D. S. *Who will an - swer, glad - ly say - ing, "Here am I, O Lord, send me."*

Loud and long the Mas - ter call - eth, Rich re-ward He of - fers free;

2 If you cannot cross the ocean
  And the heathen lands explore,
You can find the heathen nearer,
  You can help them at your door:
If you cannot speak like angels,
  If you cannot preach like Paul,
You can tell the love of Jesus,
  You can say He died for all.

3 While the souls of men are dying,
  And the Master calls for you,
Let none hear you idly saying,
  "There is nothing I can do!"
Gladly take the task He gives you,
  Let His work your pleasure be;
Answer quickly when He calleth,
  "Here am I, O Lord, send me."

194. Your Mission.

Mrs. E. H. Gates.   By permission of S. Brainard's Sons, owners of Copyright.   S. M. Grannis,

1. If you can-not on the o - cean Sail a - mong the swiftest fleet, Rocking

Your Mission.—Concluded

on the high-est bil-lows, Laughing at the storms you meet; You can

stand a-mong the sail-ors; Anchored yet with-in the bay, You can

lend a hand to help them, As they launch their boats away, As they launch their boats away.

2 If you are too weak to journey,
   Up the mountain, steep and high;
   You can stand within the valley,
   While the multitudes go by;
   You can chant in happy measure,
   As they slowly pass along;
   Though they may forget the singer,
   They will not forget the song.

3 If you cannot in the harvest
   Garner up the richest sheaves,
   Many a grain, both ripe and golden
   May the careless reapers leave.
   Go and glean among the briers,
   Growing rank against the wall,
   For it may be that their shadow
   Hides the heaviest wheat of all.

4 If you have not gold and silver
   Ever ready to command;
   If you cannot toward the needy
   Reach an ever open hand,
   You can visit the afflicted,
   O'er the erring you can weep:
   You can be a true disciple
   Sitting at the Saviour's feet.

5 Do not, then, stand idly waiting,
   For some greater work to do;
   Time moves on with rapid motion,
   Life and death are both in view;
   Go and toil in any vineyard,
   Do not fear to do or dare;
   If you want a field of labor,
   You can find it any where.

195. Quiet, Lord, my Froward Heart.

Rev. J. NEWTON.   (KÜCKEN.)   F. W. KUCKEN. Arr. by H. P. MAIN.

1. Qui-et, Lord, my froward heart; Make me teach-a-ble and mild, Upright, simple, free from art,
2. What Thou shalt to-day provide, Let me as a child receive; What to-morrow may be-tide,
3. As a lit-tle child re-lies On a care beyond his own, Knows he's neither strong nor wise,

Make me as a weaned child,—From distrust and en-vy free, Pleased with all that pleases Thee
Calmly to Thy wisdom leave: 'Tis enough that Thou wilt care; Why should I the burden bear?
Fears to stir a step a-lone; Let me thus with Thee abide, As my Father, Guard, and Guide.

196. Blessed Saviour! Thee I Love.

GEO. DUFFIELD, D.D.   (SPANISH HYMN.)   ANON.

1. Blessed Saviour! Thee I love, All my other joys a-bove; All my hopes in Thee a-bide;
2. Once a-gain beside the cross, All my gain I count but loss; Earthly pleasures fade a-way,
3. Blessed Saviour! Thine am I, Thine to live, and Thine to die; Height, or depth, or earthly power,

Thou my hope, and naught beside! Ev-er let my glo-ry be, Blessed Saviour, only Thee!
Clouds they are that hide my day; Hence, vain shadows, let me see Jesus crucified for me.
Ne'er shall hide my Saviour more; Ev-er shall my glory be, Blessed Saviour, only Thee! Amen.

197. Dear Saviour, ever at my Side.

REV F. W. FABER.   (ORIOLA.)   WM. B. BRADBURY.

1. Dear Saviour, ev - er at my side, How loving Thou must be, To leave Thy home in heaven to guard A lit - tle child like me! Thy beau - ti - ful and shin-ing face I see not, tho' so near; The sweetness of Thy soft, low voice I am too deaf to hear.

2 I cannot feel Thee touch my hand
   With pressure light and mild,
To check me, as my mother doth,
   While I am but a child;
But I have felt Thee in my thoughts
   Fighting with sin for me;
And when my heart loves God, I know
   The sweetness is from Thee.

3 And when, dear Saviour! I kneel down
   Morning and night to prayer,
Something there is within my heart
   Which tells me Thou art there;
Yes! when I pray, Thou prayest too—
   Thy prayer is all for me;
But when I sleep, Thou sleepest not,
   But watchest patiently.

198.   COMING TO CHRIST.

1 DEAR Jesus, let Thy pitying eye
   Look kindly down on me;
A sinful, weak, and helpless child,
   I come Thy child to be.

2 O blessed Saviour! take my heart,
   This sinful heart of mine,
And wash it clean in every part;
   Make me a child of Thine.

3 My sins, though great, Thou canst forgive,
   For Thou hast died for me;
Amazing love! help me, O God,
   Thine own dear child to be.

4 For Thou hast said, "Forbid them not:
   Let children come to me:"
I hear Thy voice, and now, dear Lord,
   I come Thy child to be.
                                    Anon.

199. With tearful Eyes I look around.

Rev. Hugh White, 1841.   (WOODWORTH.)   Wm. B. Bradbury.

1. With tear-ful eyes I look a-round, Life seems a dark and storm-y sea:

Yet, 'midst the gloom I hear a sound, A heavenly whisper, Come to me. *Amen.*

2 It tells me of a place of rest—
  It tells me where my | soul may | flee;
  Oh! to the weary, faint, opprest,
  How sweet the | bidding, | "Come to | me."

3 When nature shudders, loth to part
  From all I love, en- | joy, and see,
  When a faint chill steals o'er my heart,
  A sweet voice utters, | "Come to | me."

4 Come, for all else must faint and die,
  Earth is no resting | place for | thee;
  Heavenward direct thy weeping eye,
  I am thy | portion, | "Come to | me."

5 O voice of mercy! voice of love!
  In conflict, grief, and | ago- | ny,
  Support me, cheer me from above!
  And gently | whisper, | "Come to | me."

200. Come unto Me. Chant.

Hugh White, 1841.   Wm. B. Bradbury, 1853.

With tearful eyes I look around, Life seems a dark and...... | storm-y | sea: Yet, 'midst the gloom I hear a sound, A heavenly...... | whis - per, | Come to | me.

201. From every Stormy Wind that blows.

Rev. HUGH STOWELL.   (RETREAT.)   THOS. HASTINGS.

1. From ev - ery storm - y wind that blows, From ev - ery swell - ing
2. There is a place where Je - sus sheds The oil of glad - ness

tide of woes, There is a calm, a sure re - treat;
on our heads,—A place, than all be - sides, more sweet;

'Tis found be - neath the mer - cy - seat.
It is the blood-bought mer - cy - seat.   A - men.

3 There is a scene where spirits blend,
 Where friend holds fellowship with friend;
 Though sundered far, by faith they meet
 Around one common mercy-seat.

4 Oh! let my hand forget her skill,
 My tongue be silent, cold, and still,
 This throbbing heart forget to beat,
 If I forget the mercy-seat.

202

1 MY God, my Father, while I stray
 Far from my home, on life's rough way,
 Oh teach me from my heart to say,
 "Thy will be done, Thy will be done!"

2 What though in lonely grief I sigh
 For friends beloved no longer nigh;
 Submissive still would I reply,
 "Thy will be done, Thy will be done!"

3 If Thou shouldst call me to resign
 What most I prize,—it ne'er was mine;
 I only yield Thee what was Thine:
 "Thy will be done, Thy will be done!"

4 If but my fainting heart be blest
 With Thy sweet Spirit for its guest,
 My God, to Thee I leave the rest;
 "Thy will be done, Thy will be done!"

5 Renew my will from day to day;
 Blend it with Thine, and take away
 Whate'er now makes it hard to say,
 "Thy will be done, Thy will be done!"

6 Then, when on earth I breathe no more
 The prayer oft mixed with tears before,
 I'll sing, upon a happier shore,
 "Thy will be done, Thy will be done!"

Miss C. Elliott.

203. There is a Fountain filled with Blood.

W. COWPER.   (COWPER.)   LOWELL MASON.

1. There is a fountain filled with blood, Drawn from Immanuel's veins; And sinners, plunged beneath that flood, Lose all their guilt-y stains, Lose all their guilt-y stains. A - men.

2 The dying thief rejoiced to see
  That fountain in his day;
  And there may I, though vile as he,
  Wash all my sins away.

3 Dear dying Lamb, Thy precious blood
  Shall never lose its power,
  Till all the ransomed church of God
  Be saved to sin no more.

4 E'er since, by faith, I saw the stream
  Thy flowing wounds supply,
  Redeeming love has been my theme,
  And shall be, till I die.

5 Then in a nobler, sweeter song,
  I'll sing Thy power to save,
  When this poor lisping, stammering tongue
  Lies silent in the grave.

204. Fountain.

WESTERN AIR.

1. There is a fountain filled with blood, Drawn from Immanuel's veins; And sinners, plunged beneath that flood, Lose all their guilt-y stains, Lose all their guilt-y stains, Lose

Fountain.—Concluded.

all their guilty stains, And sinners, plunged beneath that flood, Lose all their guilty stains.

205. Lord, I hear of Showers of Blessing.

ELIZABETH CODNER. (EVEN ME.) WM. B. BRADBURY.

1. { Lord, I hear of showers of bless - ing Thou art scatter-ing full and free; }
   { Showers the thirst - y soul re-fresh - ing; Let some droppings fall on me, }

E - ven me. E - ven me, Let some droppings fall on me. A - men.

2 Pass me not, O gracious Father!
  Lost and sinful though I be;
  Thou might'st curse me, but the rather
  Let Thy mercy light on me.
  Even me.

3 Have I long in sin been sleeping?
  Long been slighting, grieving Thee!
  Has the world my heart been keeping,
  Oh! forgive and rescue me!
  Even me.

4 Pass me not, O mighty Spirit!
  Thou canst make the blind to see;
  Testify of Jesus' merit,
  Speak the word of peace to me.
  Even me.

206. EVEN THEE.

1 Hark! the Saviour's voice from heaven
  Speaks a pardon full and free;
  Come, and thou shalt be forgiven;
  Boundless mercy flows for thee,
  Even thee!

2 See the healing fountain springing
  From the Saviour on the tree;
  Pardon, peace, and cleansing bringing,
  Lost one, loved one, 'tis for thee,
  Even thee!

3 Come, then, now—to Jesus flying,
  From thy sin and woe be free;
  Burdened, guilty, wounded, dying,
  Gladly will He welcome Thee,
  Even thee!

4 Every sin shall be forgiven;
  Thou through grace a child shalt be;
  Child of God, and heir of heaven,
  Yes, a mansion waits for thee,
  Even thee!

207. The Precious Name.

Mrs. LYDIA BAXTER.   W. H. DOANE, by per.

1. Take the name of Je - sus with you, Child of sor - row and of woe—
2. Take the name of Je - sus ev - er, As a shield from ev - ery snare;

It will joy and com - fort give you, Take it, then, where'er you go.
If tempt - a - tions 'round you gath - er, Breathe that ho - ly name in pray'r.

CHORUS.

Pre - cious name, O how sweet! Hope of earth and joy of

Precious name, O how sweet,

heaven, Precious name, O how sweet— Hope of earth and joy of heav'n.

Copyright, 1871, by Biglow & Main.   Precious name, O how sweet, how sweet,

3 Oh! the precious name of Jesus;
　How it thrills our souls with joy,
When His loving arms receive us,
　And His songs our tongues employ!

4 At the name of Jesus bowing,
　Falling prostrate at His feet,
King of kings in heav'n we'll crown Him,
　When our journey is complete.

120

208. Wondrous Love.

Mrs. MARTHA M. STOCKTON, 1871.
WM. G. FISCHER, by per.

1. God loved the world of sin - ners lost And ru - ined by the
2. E'en now by faith I claim Him mine, The ris - en Son of

fall; Sal - va - tion full, at high - est cost, He of - fers free to all.
God; Re - demp-tion by His death I find, And cleansing through the blood.

CHORUS.

Oh, 'twas love, 'twas wondrous love! The love of God to me; It

brought my Sav - iour from a - bove, To die on Cal - va - ry.

3 Love brings the glorious fulness in,
   And to His saints makes known
   The blessed rest from inbred sin,
   Through faith in Christ alone.

4 Believing souls, rejoicing go;
   There shall to you be given
   A glorious foretaste, here below,
   Of endless life in heaven.

209. I love to Think, though I am Young.

E. PAXTON HOOD.   (ARLINGTON.)   THOMAS A. ARNE. 1762.

1. I love to think, tho' I am young My Saviour was a child; That Jesus walked this earth a-
2. He kept His Father's word of truth, As I am taught to do: And while He walked the paths of
3. I love to think that He who spake, And made the blind to see, And called the sleeping dead to
4. That He who wore the thorny crown, And tasted death's despair, Had a kind mother like my

long, With feet all un - de - filed.
youth, He walked in wisdom too.
wake, Was once a child like me.
own, And knew her love and care. *A-men.*

5 I know 'twas all for love of me
    That He became a child,
  And left the heavens so fair to see,
    And trod earth's pathway wild.

6 Then, Saviour, who wast once a child,
    A child may come to Thee;
  And oh! in all Thy mercy mild,
    Dear Saviour, come to me.

210. Children of the Heavenly King.

J. CENNICK.   (PLEYEL'S HYMN.)   I. PLEYEL.

1. Children of the heavenly King, As ye journey, sweetly sing; Sing your Saviour's worthy
2. Ye are traveling home to God In the way the fa - thers trod; They are happy now and

praise, Glorious in His works and ways.
ye   Soon their happi - ness shall see. *A-men.*

3 Fear not, brethren; joyful stand
    On the borders of your land;
  Jesus Christ, your Father's Son,
    Bids you undismayed go on.

4 Lord, submissive make us go,
    Gladly leaving all below;
  Only Thou our Leader be,
    And we still will follow Thee.

122

211. Shall we gather at the River?

R. Lowry, 1864.   Rev. Robert Lowry, by per.

1. Shall we gath - er at the riv - er Where bright an - gel feet have trod;
2. On the mar - gin of the riv - er, Wash - ing up its sil - ver spray,
3. Ere we reach the shin - ing riv - er, Lay we ev - ery bur - den down;

With its crys - tal tide for - ev - er Flow-ing by the throne of God?
We will walk and wor - ship ev - er, All the hap - py gold - en day.
Grace our spir - its will de - liv - er, And pro - vide a robe and crown.

Chorus.

Yes, we'll gath-er at the riv - er, The beau - ti-ful, the beau-ti - ful riv - er, —

Gath - er with the saints at the riv - er That flows by the throne of God.

4 At the smiling of the river,
   Mirror of the Saviour's face,
   Saints whom death will never sever
   Lift their songs of saving grace.

5 Soon we'll reach the silver river,
   Soon our pilgrimage will cease;
   Soon our happy hearts will quiver
   With the melody of peace.

123

212. Close to Thee.

FANNY J. CROSBY.

S. J. VAIL, by per.

1. Thou my ev - er - last - ing por - tion, More than friend or life to me,
2. Not for ease or world-ly pleas-ure, Nor for fame my prayer shall be;
3. Lead me thro' the vale of shad-ows, Bear me o'er life's fit - ful sea;

All a - long my pil - grim jour - ney, Sav - iour, let me walk with Thee.
Glad - ly will I toil and suf - fer, On - ly let me walk with Thee.
Then the gate of life e - ter - nal, May I en - ter, Lord, with Thee.

REFRAIN.

Close to Thee, close to Thee, close to Thee, close to Thee; All a -
Close to Thee, close to Thee, close to Thee, close to Thee; Glad - ly
Close to Thee, close to Thee, close to Thee, close to Thee; Then the

long my pil - grim journ - ey, Sav - iour, let me walk with Thee.
will I toil and suf - fer, On - ly let me walk with Thee.
gate of life e - ter - nal, May I en - ter, Lord, with Thee.

213. Bless Me Now.

ALEXANDER CLARK, D.D.

Rev. ROBERT LOWRY, by per.

1. Heaven-ly Fa - ther, bless me now; At the cross of Christ I bow;
2. Now, O Lord! this ver - y hour, Send Thy grace and show Thy power;
3. Now, just now, for Je - sus' sake, Lift the clouds, the fet - ters break;

Take my guilt and grief a - way; Hear and heal me now, I pray.
While I rest up - on Thy word, Come and bless me now, O Lord!
While I look, · and as I cry, Touch and cleanse me ere I die.

REFRAIN.

Bless me now, bless me now, Heaven - ly Fa - ther, bless me now.

Copyright, 1873, by Biglow & Main.

214. **CONSECRATION.**

1 TAKE my life and let it be
   Consecrated, Lord, to Thee;
   Take my hands and let them move
   At the impulse of Thy love.

REF.—All to Thee, all to Thee,
   Consecrated, Lord, to Thee.

2 Take my feet and let them be
   Swift and beautiful for Thee;
   Take my voice and let me sing
   Always—only—for my King. REF.

3 Take my lips and let them be
   Filled with messages from Thee;

Take my silver and my gold,
Not a mite would I withhold. REF.

4 Take my moments and my days,
   Let them flow in endless praise;
   Take my intellect and use
   Every power as Thou shalt choose. REF.

5 Take my will and make it Thine,
   It shall be no longer mine;
   Take my heart, it is Thine own,
   It shall be Thy royal throne. REF.

6 Take my love, my God, I pour
   At Thy feet its treasure store;
   Take myself, and I will be
   Ever, only, all for Thee. REF.

Frances R. Havergal.

215. Sweet Saviour, bless us ere we go.

M. COLLINS.   (BENEDICTION.)   J. BARNSY.

1. Sweet Sav - iour, bless us ere we go; Thy word in - to our
2. Grant us, dear Lord, from e - vil ways True ab - so - lu - tion

minds in - still; And make our luke - warm hearts to glow With
and re - lease; And bless us, more than in past days, With

low - ly love and fer - vent will. Thro' life's long day and
pur - i - ty and in - ward peace. Thro' life's long day and

death's dark night, O gen - tle Je - sus, be our Light.
death's dark night, O gen - tle Je - sus, be our Light. A - men.

3 Do more than pardon; give us joy,
Sweet fear, and sober liberty,
And simple hearts without alloy
That only long to be like Thee.

4 Labor is sweet, for Thou hast toiled;
And care is light, for Thou hast cared;
Ah! never let our works be soiled
With strife, or by deceit ensnared.

126

216. Jesus of Nazareth passeth by.

Miss EMMA CAMPBELL.

T. E. PERKINS, by per.

1. { What means this ea-ger, anxious throng, Which moves with busy haste along— }
{ These wondrous gatherings day by day? What means this strange com-(*Omit*.) } { motion, say?

2. { Who is this Je-sus? why should He The cit-y move so might-i-ly? }
{ A pass-ing stranger, has He skill To move the mul-ti-(*Omit*........) } { tude at will?

In ac-cents hushed the throng re-ply: "Je-sus of Naz-a-reth pass-eth by;"
A-gain the stir-ing tones re-ply: "Je-sus of Naz-a-reth pass-eth by;"

In ac-cents hushed the throng re-ply: "Je-sus of Naz-a-reth pass-eth by."
A-gain the stir-ring tones re-ply: "Je-sus of Naz-a-reth pass-eth by."

3 Jesus! 'tis He who once below
Man's pathway trod, 'mid pain and woe;
And burdened hearts, where'er He came,
Brought out their sick, and deaf, and lame.
Blind men rejoiced to hear the cry:
"Jesus of Nazareth passeth by."

4 Again He comes; From place to place
His holy footprints we can trace,
He pauses at our threshold—nay,
He enters—condescends to stay.
Shall we not gladly raise the cry,
"Jesus of Nazareth passeth by."

5 Ho! all ye heavy-laden come!
Here's pardon, comfort, rest, and home;
Ye wanderers from a Father's face,
Return, accept His proffered grace,
Ye tempted, there's a refuge nigh:
"Jesus of Nazareth passeth by."

6 But if you still this call refuse,
And all His wondrous love abuse,
Soon will He sadly from you turn,
Your bitter prayer for pardon spurn.
"Too late! too late!" will be the cry—
"Jesus of Nazareth *has passed* by."

Now the Day is over.

(EMMELAR.)

Rev. S. Baring-Gould.   J. Barnby, 1868.

1. Now the day is o - ver, Night is draw - ing nigh,
2. Je - sus, give the wea - ry Calm and sweet re - pose

Shad - ows of the eve - ning Steal a - cross the sky.
With Thy tend - 'rest bless - ing May our eye - lids close.

bless-ing May our eye - - - lids close.

3 Grant to little children
  Visions bright of Thee,
  Guard the sailors tossing
  On the deep blue sea.

4 Through the long night-watches
  May Thine Angels spread
  Their white wings above me,
  Watching round my bed.

5 When the morning wakens,
  Then may I arise
  Pure and fresh and sinless
  In Thy Holy Eyes.

218. A PRAYER TO JESUS.

1 Jesus, Lord and Master,
  At Thy sacred feet,
  Here with hearts rejoicing
  See Thy children meet;

2 Often have we left Thee,
  Often gone astray,
  Keep us, mighty Saviour,
  In the narrow way.

3 All our days direct us
  In the way we go,
  Lead us on victorious
  Over every foe;

4 Bid Thine angels shield us
  When the storm-clouds lower,
  Pardon Thou and save us
  In the last dread hour.

5 Then with saints and angels
  May we join above,
  Offering endless praises
  At Thy throne of love.
                              Anon.

219. PRAISE TO CHRIST.

1 Saviour, blessed Saviour,
  Listen while we sing;
  Hearts and voices raising,
  Praises to our King;

2 All we have to offer,
  All we hope to be,
  Body, soul and spirit,
  All, we yield to Thee.

3 Nearer, ever nearer,
  Christ, we draw to Thee,
  Deep in adoration
  Bending low the knee:

4 Thou for our redemption,
  Cam'st on earth to die;
  Thou, that we might follow,
  Hast gone up on high.

5 Great and ever greater
  Are Thy mercies here,
  True and everlasting
  Are the glories there,

6 Where no pain nor sorrow,
  Toil nor care is known;
  Where the angel-legions
  Circle round Thy Throne. .
                         Godfrey Thring.

220.   Near the Cross.

FANNY J. CROSBY.   W. H. DOANE.

1. Je - sus, keep me near the cross, There a pre - cious foun - tain,
2. Near the Cross, a trem - bling soul, Love and mer - cy found me;
3. Near the Cross! oh, Lamb of God, Bring its scenes be - fore me;
4. Near the Cross I'll watch and wait Hop - ing, trust - ing ev - er,

Free to all, a heal - ing stream, Flows from Calva - ry's moun - tain.
There the Bright and Morn - ing Star Shed its beams a - round me.
Help me walk from day to day With its shad - ow o'er me.
Till I reach the heaven-ly land Just be - yond the riv - er.

CHORUS.

In the Cross, In the Cross, Be my glo - ry ev - er;

Till my rap - tured soul shall find Rest be - yond the riv - er.

221. One more Day's Work for Jesus.

Miss ANNA WARNER. 1864.   Rev. ROBERT LOWRY, by per.

1. One more day's work for Je-sus, One less of life for me! But heav'n is nearer,
2. One more day's work for Je-sus, How glorious is my King! 'Tis joy, not du-ty,
3. One more day's work for Je-sus, How sweet the work has been, To tell the sto-ry,

And Christ is dear-er Than yes-ter-day to me; His love and light
To speak His beau-ty; My soul mounts on the wing At the mere tho't
To show the glo-ry, Where Christ's flock en-ter in! How it did shine

CHORUS.

Fill all my soul to-night. One more day's work for Je-sus, One more day's work for
How Christ my life has bought.
In this poor heart of mine.

Je-sus, One more day's work for Je-sus, One less of life for me.

4 One more day's work for Jesus—
  Oh, yes, an earnest day;
For heaven shines clearer,
And rest comes nearer,
At each step of the way;
  And Christ in all—
  Before His face I fall.

5 Oh, blessed work for Jesus;
  Oh, rest at Jesus' feet!
There toil seems pleasure,
My wants are treasure,
And pain for Him is sweet,
  Lord, if I may,
  I'll serve another day!

222.   # Lord Jesus! I belong to Thee.

ANON.   Rev. G. G. PHIPPS.

1. Lord, from the depths to Thee I cry, To Thee I lift my tear-ful eye: My Sav-iour! let me feel Thee nigh,
2. No home have I in this wide waste, O'er which with trem-bling steps I haste, The joys at Thy right hand to taste,
3. Oh, then be Thou each hour our guide; Ne'er let my faith-less foot-steps slide; But keep me by Thy wound-ed side.

CHORUS.

Lord Je-sus! I be-long to Thee. Lord, Thou hast bought me, I'm not mine own, Thy precious blood to my heart is whispering "Thine, Thine alone."

4 In dark temptation's trial hour,   ·
   When Satan bends his utmost power,
   My Saviour! be my refuge tower,
   Lord Jesus! I belong to Thee.

5 And when at length life's pulses fail,
   And weary feet tread death's dim vale,
   Breathe to my heart Thine oft-told tale,
   Lord Jesus! I belong to Thee.

223.   Sparkling and Bright.

Mrs. MARY S. B. DANA.   (TEMPERANCE.)   J. B. TAYLOR, 1890.

1. Sparkling and bright, in its li-quid light, Is the wa-ter in our glass - es;
2. Bet - ter than gold, is the wa-ter cold, From the crys-tal fountain flow - ing;
3. Sor - row has fled from the hearts that bled, Of the weeping wife and moth - er,

'Twill give you health, 'Twill give you wealth, Ye lads and ro - sy lass - es !
A calm de-light, both day and night, To hap-py homes be - stow - ing:
They have giv-en up the poisoned cup, Son, husband, daughter, broth - er.

CHORUS.

Oh, then, re - sign your ru - by wine, Each smil - ing son and daugh - ter,

There's nothing so good for the youthful blood, Or sweet as the sparkling wa - ter.

224. Friends of Freedom.

1. Friends of freedom! swell the song; Young and old, the strain prolong, Make the temp'rance
2. Shrink not when the foe appears; Spurn the coward's guilty fears; Hear the shrieks, be-

ar - my strong, And on to vic - to - ry. Lift your ban - ners, let them wave;
hold the tears Of ru - ined fam - i - lies! Raise the cry in ev - ery spot—

Onward march the world to save; Who would fill a drunkard's grave, And bear his infamy?
Touch not—Taste not—Handle not, Who would be a drunken sot, The worst of mis - e - ries?

3 Give the aching bosom rest;
  Carry joy to every breast;
Make the wretched drunkard blest,
    By living soberly.
Raise the glorious watchword high—
" Touch not—Taste not—till you die!
Let the echo reach the sky,
    And earth keep jubilee.

4 God of mercy ! hear us plead,
  For Thy help we intercede !
See how many bosoms bleed !
    And heal them speedily.
Hasten, Lord, the happy day,
When beneath thy gentle ray,
Temp'rance all the world shall sway,
    And reign triumphantly.

225. I hear thy Welcome Voice.

Rev. L. Hartsough.　　　　　　　　　　　　Rev. Lewis Hartsough, by per.

1. I hear Thy wel-come voice, That calls me, Lord, to Thee; For
2. Tho' com-ing weak and vile, Thou dost my strength as-sure; Thou
3. 'Tis Je-sus calls me on To per-fect faith and love, To

cleans-ing in Thy pre-cious blood, That flowed on Cal - va - ry.
dost my vile - ness ful - ly cleanse, Till spot - less all, and pure.
per - fect hope, and peace, and trust, For earth and heaven a - bove.

Chorus.

I am com-ing, Lord! Com-ing now to Thee!

Wash me, cleanse me, in the blood that flowed on Cal - va - ry!

4 And He the witness gives
　To loyal hearts and free,
That every promise is fulfilled,
　If faith but brings the plea.

5 All hail! atoning blood!
　All hail! redeeming grace!
All hail! the gift of Christ, our Lord,
　Our Strength and Righteousness.

226. I am Praying for You.

S. O'MALEY CLUFF.

IRA D. SANKEY, by per.

1. I have a Saviour, He's pleading in glo - ry, A dear, lov-ing Sav - iour, tho'
2. I have a Father: to me He has giv - en A hope for e - ter - ni - ty,
3. I have a peace: it is calm as a riv - er— A peace that the friends of this
4. When Je - sus has found you, tell others the sto - ry, That my lov - ing Sav - iour is

earth-friends be few; And now He is watching in ten - der-ness o er me, And
bless - ed and true; And soon will He call me to meet Him in heav - en, But
world nev - er knew; My Sav - iour a - lone is its Au - thor and Giv - er, And
your Saviour too; Then pray that your Sav - iour may bring them to glo - ry, And

CHORUS.

oh, that my Sav - iour were your Sav-iour too! For you I am pray - ing, For
oh, that He'd let me bring you with me too!
oh, could I know it was giv - en to you!
prayer will be answered—'twas answered for you!

you I am pray - ing, For you I am pray - ing, I'm pray-ing for you!

227. Sun of my Soul, Thou Saviour dear.

Rev. J. Keble.   (HURSLEY.)   Peter Ritter.

1. Sun of my soul! Thou Saviour dear, It is not night if Thou be near; Oh, may no earth-born cloud a-
2. When soft the dews of kindly sleep My wearied eyelids gently steep, Be my last tho't,—how sweet to

rise To hide Thee from Thy servant's eyes!
rest. Forever on my Saviour's breast. A-men.

3 Abide with me from morn till eve,
For without Thee I cannot live;
Abide with me when night is nigh,
For without Thee I dare not die.

4 Be near to bless me when I wake,
Ere through the world my way I take;
Abide with me till in Thy love
I lose myself in heaven above.

228. CHRIST KNOCKING AT THE DOOR.

1 Behold a Stranger at the door!
He gently knocks, has knocked before;
Has waited long, is waiting still;
You treat no other friend so ill.

2 Oh, lovely attitude! He stands
With melting heart and laden hands;
Oh, matchless kindness! and He shows
This matchless kindness to His foes.

3 But will He prove a friend indeed?
He will, the very friend you need—
The Friend of sinners; yes, 'tis He,
With garments dyed on Calvary.

4 Rise, touched with gratitude divine,
Turn out His enemy and thine,
That soul-destroying monster sin,
And let the heavenly Stranger in.
J. Grigg.

229. Come, sound His praise abroad.

I. Watts.   (SILVER STREET.)   I. Smith.

1. Come, sound His praise a-broad, And hymns of glo-ry sing: Je-ho-vah

is the sov-'reign God, The u-ni-ver-sal King. A-men.

Come, sound His praise.—Concluded.

2 He formed the deeps unknown;
He gave the seas their bound;
The watery worlds are all His own,
And all the solid ground.

3 Come, worship at His throne,
Come, bow before the Lord:
We are His work, and not our own;
He formed us by His word.

4 To-day attend His voice,
Nor dare provoke His rod;
Come, like the people of His choice,
And own our gracious God.

230. FAITH AND COURAGE.

1 GIVE to the winds thy fears;
Hope, and be undismayed;

God hears thy sighs and counts thy tears;
God shall lift up thy head.

2 Through waves, and clouds, and storms,
He gently clears thy way;
Wait thou His time; so shall this night
Soon end in joyous day.

3 What though thou rulest not!
Yet heaven, and earth, and hell
Proclaim, God sitteth on the throne,
And ruleth all things well.

4 Far, far above thy thought
His counsel shall appear,
When fully He the work has wrought,
That caused thy needless fear.

J. Wesley.

231. My Soul, be on thy Guard.

GEORGE HEATH. (LABAN.) LOWELL MASON.

1. My soul, be on thy guard! Ten thou-sand foes a-rise; And
2. Oh, watch, and fight, and pray! The bat-tle ne'er give o'er; Re-

hosts of sin are press-ing hard To draw thee from the skies.
new it bold-ly ev-ery day, And help di-vine im-plore. A-men.

3 Ne'er think the vict'ry won,
Nor lay thine armor down;
Thine arduous work will not be done,
Till thou obtain thy crown.

4 Fight on, my soul, till death
Shall bring thee to thy God!
He'll take thee at thy parting breath,
Up to His blest abode.

232. COME, HOLY SPIRIT.

1 COME, Holy Spirit, come!
Let Thy bright beams arise;
Dispel the sorrow from our minds,
The darkness from our eyes.

2 Convince us of our sin;
Then lead to Jesus' blood,

And to our wondering view reveal
The mercies of our God.

3 Revive our drooping faith,
Our doubts and fears remove,
And kindle in our breasts the flame
Of never-dying love.

4 'Tis thine to cleanse the heart,
To sanctify the soul,
To pour fresh life in every part,
And new-create the whole.

5 Come, Holy Spirit, come;
Our minds from bondage free;
Then shall we know, and praise, and love,
The Father, Son, and Thee.

J. Hart.

233. Jerusalem, the Golden.

Rev. JOHN MASON NEALE, D. D..   ALEX. EWING, 1868.

1. Je - ru - sa - lem, the gold - en! With milk and hon - ey blest; Beneath thy con - tem -
2. They stand, those halls of Zi - on, All ju - bi - lant with song, And bright with many an
3. And they who with their Lead - er Have conquered in the fight, For - ev - er and for -
4. O sweet and bless-ed coun - try! The home of God's e - lect! O sweet and bless - ed

pla - tion Sink heart and voice op - prest. I know not, oh, I know not What
an - gel And all the mar - tyr throng, There is the throne of Da - vid, And
ev - er, Are clad in robes of white. O land that seest no sor - row! O
coun-try That eag - er hearts ex - pect! Je - sus, in mer - cy bring us To

ho - ly joys are there, What ra-dian-cy of glo - ry, What bliss beyond compare.
there, from toil released, The shout of them that triumph, The song of them that feast.
state that fear'st no strife! O roy - al land of flow-ers! O realm and home of life!
that dear land of rest; Who art, with God the Father And Spir-it, ev - er blest. Amen.

234.

1 Thou chief among ten thousand.
  Who can with thee compare?
Thou hast my soul's devotion,—
  Supreme, Thou reignest there:
I know no life divided
  O blessed Lord, from Thee;
In Thee is life provided
  For all mankind and me.

2 O hold Thou up my goings,
  And lead from strength to strength,
That unto Thee in Zion
  I may appear at length :

O make my spirit worthy
  To join the ransomed throng ;
O teach my lips to utter
  That everlasting song.

3 O give that last, best blessing,
  That even saints can know,
To follow in Thy footsteps
  Wherever Thou dost go:
Not wisdom, might or glory
  I ask to win above;
I ask for Thee, Thee only,
  O Thou Eternal Love !

235. From Greenland's Icy Mountains.

Rev. R. Heber. (MISSIONARY HYMN.) Lowell Mason.

1. { From Greenland's i - cy mountains, From In - dia's co - ral strand, }
{ Where Af - ric's sun - ny foun - tains [Omit................ } Roll down their gold - en sand; From many an

an - cient riv - er, From many a palm - y plain, They call us to de - liv - er Their land from er - ror's chain.

2 What though the spicy breezes
  Blow soft o'er Ceylon's isle;
Though every prospect pleases,
  And only man is vile;
In vain with lavish kindness
  The gifts of God are strown;
The heathen in his blindness,
  Bows down to wood and stone!

3 Shall we, whose souls are lighted
  With wisdom from on high,—
Shall we, to men benighted,
  The lamp of life deny?
Salvation, oh, salvation!
  The joyful sound proclaim,
Till earth's remotest nation
  Has learned Messiah's name.

4 Waft, waft, ye winds, his story,
  And you, ye waters, roll,
Till, like a sea of glory,
  It spreads from pole to pole;
Till o'er our ransomed nature
  The Lamb for sinners slain,
Redeemer, King, Creator,
  In bliss returns to reign!

236.

1 I lay my sins on Jesus,
  The spotless Lamb of God;
He bears them all, and frees us
  From the accursed load:
I bring my guilt to Jesus,
  To wash my crimson stains
White, in His blood most precious,
  Till not a stain remains.

2 I lay my wants on Jesus;
  All fulness dwells in Him;
He healeth my diseases,
  He doth my soul redeem:
I lay my griefs on Jesus,
  My burdens and my cares;
He from them all releases,
  He all my sorrows shares.

3 I rest my soul on Jesus
  This weary soul of mine;
His right hand me embraces,
  I on His breast recline:
I love the name of Jesus,
  Immanuel, Christ, the Lord;
Like fragrance on the breezes,
  His name abroad is poured.

4 I long to be like Jesus,
  Meek, loving, lowly, mild;
I long to be like Jesus,
  The Father's holy child:
I long to be with Jesus
  Amid the heavenly throng,
To sing with saints his praises,
  And learn the angel's song.

Rev. H. Bonar.

237.   Immanuel's Land.

ANNIE ROSS COUSIN, 1857.   (RUTHERFORD.)   CHAS. D'URHAN, 1845.

1. The sands of time are sink - ing, The dawn of heav - en breaks,
2. Oh! Christ He is the foun - tain, The deep, sweet well of love;
3. Oh! I am my Be - lov - ed's, And my Be - lov - ed's mine,

The sum - mer morn I've sighed for, The fair, sweet morn a - wakes, Oh,
The streams of earth I've tast - ed, More deep I'll drink a - bove, There
He brings a poor vile sin - ner, In - to His house. di - vine. Up -

dark hath been the mid - night, But day - spring is at hand,
to an o - cean ful - ness, His mer . cy doth ex - pund,
on the Rock of A - ges, My soul redeemed, shall stand,

And glo - ry, glo - ry dwell - eth In Im - man - uel's land.
And glo - ry, glo - ry dwell - eth In Im - man - uel's land.
Where glo - ry, glo - ry dwell - eth In Im - man - uel's land. A-men.

238. O, do not be Discouraged.

Rev. JOHN A. GRANADE, (1770—1806), 1803, alt.

Arr. by HUBERT P. MAIN.

1. O, do not be discouraged, For Je-sus is your Friend, O do not be discouraged,
2. Fight on, ye lit-tle soldiers, The battle you shall win, Fight on, ye lit-tle soldiers,
3. And when the conflict's o - ver, Be-fore Him you shall stand; And when the conflict's over,

S.

For Je - sus is your Friend: He will give you grace to conquer, He will give you grace to
The bat - tle you shall win; For the Saviour is your Captain, For the Saviour is your
Be - fore Him you shall stand: You shall sing His praise for-ev-er, You shall sing His praise for-

D. S.—*Yes, I'm glad I'm in this ar - my, Yes, I'm glad I'm in this*

FINE. CHORUS.

conquer, And keep you to the end. I am glad I'm in this ar - my, Yes, I'm
Captain, And He has vanished sin.
ev - er, In Ca - naan's happy land.

ar - my, And I'll bat - tle for the school.

D. S.

glad I'm in 'this ar - my, Yes, I'm glad I'm in this ar - my, And I'll bat-tle for the school.

239. Saviour, Breathe an Evening blessing.

JAMES EDMESTON. (STOCKWELL.) DARIUS ELIOT JONES, 1846.

1. Saviour, breathe an evening blessin, Ere repose our spirits seal; Sin and want we come con-
2. Though destruction walk around us, Tho' the arrows past us fly, Angel guards from Thee sur-

fess-ing : Thou canst save and Thou canst heal.
round us, We are safe if Thou art nigh.

3 Though the night be dark and dreary,
   Darkness cannot hide from Thee;
Thou art He who, never weary,
   Watchest where Thy people be.

4 Should swift death this night o'ertake us,
   And our couch become our tomb,
May the morn in heaven awake us,
   Clad in light and deathless bloom.

240. EVENING HYMN.

1 SILENTLY the shades of evening
   Gather round my lowly door;
Silently they bring before me
   Faces I shall see no more.

2 O the lost, the unforgotten,
   'Though the world be oft forgot !
O the shrouded and the lonely,
   In our hearts they perish not !

3 Living in the silent hours,
   Where our spirits only blend,
They, unlinked with earthly trouble,
   We, still hoping for its end.

4 How such holy memories cluster,
   Like the stars when storms are past,
Pointing up to that fair heaven
   We may hope to gain at last.
              Christopher C. Cox, 1841.

241. Now to the Lord a Noble Song.

I. WATTS. (WARE.) GEO. KINGSLEY.

1. Now to the Lord a noble song ! Awake, my soul ! awake, my tongue ! Hosanna to th' eternal
2. See where it shines in Jesus' face,—The brightest image of His grace ! God, in the person of His

name, And all His boundless love proclaim.
Son, Hath all His mightiest works outdone.

3 Grace !—'tis a sweet, a charming theme:
   My thoughts rejoice at Jesus' name:
Ye angels ! dwell upon the sound:
   Ye heavens ! reflect it to the ground.

4 Oh, may I reach that happy place,
   Where He unveils His lovely face,
Where all His beauties you behold,
   And sing His name to harps of gold.

242. Jesus is Mighty to Save.

Mrs. ANNIE WITTENMYER.

WM. G. FISCHER, by per.

1. All glo - ry to Je - sus be given, That life and sal - va - tion are free;
2. From the dark-ness and sin and despair, Out in - to the light of His love,
3. Oh, the rapturous heights of His love, The measure - less depths of His grace.
4. In Him all my wants are sup - plied, His love makes my heav- en be - low,

And all may be wash'd and for - given, And Je - sus can save ev - en me.
He has brought me, and made me an heir, To kingdoms and mansions a - bove.
My soul all His full-ness would prove, And live in His lov - ing em - brace.
And free - ly His blood is ap - plied, His blood that makes whit-er than snow.

CHORUS.

Yes, Je - sus is mighty to save, ... And all His sal - va - tion may know; . . . . . .
is might-y to save, sal - va - tion may know;

On His bo - som I lean, And His blood makes me clean, For His blood can wash whiter than snow.

243.

Lead, Kindly Light.

(LUX BENIGNA.)

Rev. John Henry Newman, 1833.   Rev. J. B. Dykes.

1. Lead, Kind-ly Light, a-mid th'en-cir-cling gloom, Lead Thou me
2. I was not ev-er thus, nor prayed that Thou Shouldst lead me
3. So long Thy Power hath blest me, sure it still Will lead me

on; The night is dark, and I am far from home, Lead Thou me
on; I loved to choose and see my path; but now Lead Thou me
on; O'er moor and fen, o'er crag and tor-rent, till The night is

on. Keep Thou my feet; I do not ask to see
on! I loved the gar-ish day, and spite of fears,
gone, And with the morn those an-gel fa-ces smile

The dis-tant scene: one step e-nough for me.
Pride ruled my will; re-mem-ber not past years!
Which I have loved long since, and lost a-while!

144

244.

To God be the Glory.

FANNY J. CROSBY.

W. H. DOANE, by per.

1. To God be the glo-ry, great things He hath done, So loved He the world that He
2. O per-fect re-demption, the purchase of blood, To ev-ery be-liev-er the
3. Great things He hath taught us, great things He hath done, And great our rejoicing thro'

gave us His Son, Who yield-ed His life an a-tone-ment for sin, And
prom-ise of God; The vil-est of-fend-er who tru-ly believes, That
Je-sus the Son; But pur-er, and high-er, and great-er will be Our

D. S.—*O come to the Fa-ther, thro' Je-sus the Son, And*

FINE. REFRAIN.

opened the Life Gate that all may go in. Praise the Lord, praise the Lord, Let the
moment from Je-sus a par-don receives.
wonder, our transport when Je-sus we see.

give Him the glo-ry, great things He hath done.

D. S.

earth hear His voice, Praise the Lord, praise the Lord, Let the peo-ple re-joice;

245. When all Thy Mercies, O my God.

J. ADDISON.   (GENEVA.)   JOHN COLE, 1801.

1 When all Thy mercies, O...... my God! My rising soul sur-veys, Transport-ed

When all Thy mercies, O my God!

When all Thy mercies, O my God!   Trans

with the view, I'm lost In won - der, love, and praise. A - men.

ported with the view, I'm lost

2 Unnumbered comforts, to my soul,
  Thy tender care bestowed,
Before my infant heart conceived
  From whom those comforts flowed.

3 When in the slippery paths of youth,
  With heedless steps, I ran,
Thine arm, unseen, conveyed me safe,
  And led me up to man.

4 Ten thousand, thousand precious gifts
  My daily thanks employ;

Nor is the least a cheerful heart,
  That tastes those gifts with joy.

5 Through every period of my life,
  Thy goodness I'll pursue;
And after death, in distant worlds,
  The glorious theme renew.

6 Through all eternity, to Thee
  A joyful song I'll raise:
For, oh, eternity's too short
  To utter all Thy praise!

246. All hail the power of Jesus' name!

E. PERRONET, 1780.   (CORONATION.)   OLIVER HOLDEN.

1. All hail the power of Je - sus' name! Let an - gels prostrate fall! Bring
2. Crown Him, ye mar - tyrs of our God, Who from His al - tar call; Ex -

All hail the power of Jesus' name.—Concluded.

forth the roy - al ' di - a - dem, And crown Him Lord of all; Bring
tol the stem of Jes - se's rod, And crown Him Lord of all; Ex -

forth the roy - al di - a - dem, And crown Him Lord of all.
tol the stem of Jes - se's rod, And crown Him Lord of all. A - men.

3 Ye chosen seed of Israel's race,
Ye ransomed from the fall;
Hail Him, who saves you by His grace,
And crown Him Lord of all.

4 Sinners, whose love can ne'er forget
The wormwood and the gall;
Go, spread your trophies at His feet.
And crown Him Lord of all.

5 Let every kindred, every tribe,
On this terrestrial ball,
To Him all majesty ascribe,
And crown Him Lord of all.

6 Oh, that with yonder sacred throng,
We at His feet may fall;
We'll join the everlasting song,
And crown Him Lord of all.

247.   Miles Lane.   C. M.

E. PERRONET.   W. SHRUBSOLE.

1. All hail the power of Je - sus' name! Let an - gels prostrate fall; Bring forth the royal

di - a - dem, And crown Him, crown Him, crown Him, crown Him Lord of all.

147

248.   **Hosanna to the Lamb of God.**

ISAAC WATTS   (VICTORY.)   GERMAN.

1. Des - cend from heav'n, Im - mor - tal Dove; Stoop down and take us on Thy wings;
2. Be - yond, beyond this low - er sky, Up where e - ter - nal ag - es roll,

And mount, and bear us far a - bove The reach of these in - fer - ior things;
Where sol - id pleasures nev - er die, And fruits im-mor - tal feast the soul.

CHORUS.

Glo - ry, glo - ry let us sing, While heav'n and earth with glo - ry ring,

Ho - san - na; Ho - san - na! Ho - san - na to the Lamb of God.

3 O for a sight, a pleasing sight,
   Of our Almighty Father's throne!
There sits our Saviour crowned with light,
   Clothed in a body like our own.

4 Adoring saints around Him stand,
   And thrones and powers before Him fall;
The God shines gracious through the man,
   And sheds sweet glories on them all.

Lord of all being; throned afar.

O. W. HOLMES.   (LOUVAN.)   V. C. TAYLOR.

1. Lord of all be-ing; throned a-far, Thy glo-ry
2. Sun of our life, Thy quicken-ing ray Sheds on our

flames from sun and star; Cen-tre and soul of
path the glow of day; Star of our hope, Thy

ev-ery sphere, Yet to each lov-ing heart how near!
soft-ened light Cheers the long watch-es of the night.

From Robinson's Spiritual Songs, by per. of the Century Co.

3 Our midnight is Thy smile withdrawn;
   Our noontide is thy gracious dawn;
   Our rainbow arch Thy mercy's sign,
   All, save the clouds of sin, are Thine!

4 Lord of all life, below, above,
   Whose light is truth, whose warmth is love,
   Before Thy ever-blazing throne
   We ask no lustre of our own.

5 Grant us Thy truth to make us free,
   And kindling hearts that burn for Thee,
   Till all thy living altars claim
   One holy light, one heavenly flame!

250.   FAITH AND HOPE.

1 I AM not skilled to understand,
   What God hath willed, what God hath planned,
   I only know at God's right hand,
     Stands one who is my Saviour.

2 I take God at His word and deed,
   Christ died to save me, this I read;
   And in my heart I find a need
     Of Him to be my Saviour.

3 And had there been in all this wide,
   Sad world no other soul beside,
   But only mine, yet He had died,
     That He might be my Saviour.

251. Battling for the Lord.

Mrs. M. A. KIDDER.
SEMI-CHORUS.
CHORUS.
T. E. PERKINS, by per.
SEMI-CHORUS.

1. We've list-ed in a ho-ly war, Battling for the Lord! E-ter-nal life, our
2. We've girded on our ar-mor bright, Battling for the Lord! Our Captain's word our
3. We'll stand like heroes on the field, Battling for the Lord! And in His strength we'll

CHORUS.   FULL CHORUS.

guid-ing star, Battling for the Lord! We'll work till Je-sus comes, We'll work till Je-sus
strength and might, Battling for the Lord!
nev-er yield. Battling for the Lord!

comes; We'll work till Je-sus comes, And then we'll rest at home

4 Though sin and death our way oppose,
   Battling for the Lord!
Through grace we'll conquer all our foes,
   Battling for the Lord!—Cho.

5 And when our glorious war is o'er,
   Conq'rors through the Lord!
We'll shout salvation evermore,
   Conq'rors through the Lord!—Cho.

252. To the Work.

FANNY J. CROSBY, 1871.
W. H. DOANE. by per.

1. To the work! to the work! we are ser-vants of God, Let us fol-low the
2. To the work! to the work! let the hun-gry be fed; To the fountain of
3. To the work! to the work! there is la-bor for all, For the kingdom of
4. To the work! to the work! in the strength of the Lord, And a robe and a

To the Work.—Concluded.

path that our Mas - ter has trod; With the balm of His coun - sel our
Life let the wea - ry be led; In the cross and its ban - ner our
dark - ness and er - ror shall fall; And the name of Je - ho - vah ex -
crown shall our la - bor re - ward; When the home of the faith - ful our

strength to re - new, Let us do with our might what our hands find to do.
glo - ry shall be. While we her - ald the tid - ings, "Sal - va - tion is free!"
alt - ed shall be In the loud-swell-ing chor - us, "Sal - va - tion is free!"
dwell - ing shall be, And we shout with the ran - som'd "Sal - va - tion is free!"

CHORUS.

Toil - ing on, Toil - ing on, Toil - ing on, Toil - ing

Toil-ing on, Toil-ing on, Toil-ing on,

on, Let us hope, Let us watch, And la - bor till the Master comes.

Toil-ing on, and trust, and pray,

253. Oh! how Happy are They!

C. WESLEY.
WM. ARNOLD, 1791.

1. Oh! how hap - py are they Who the Sav - iour o - bey, And have laid up their

trens-ures a - bove : Oh! what tongue can ex-press The sweet com - fort and peace

Of a soul in its ear - li - est love? Of a soul in its ear - li - est love. A-men.

2 It was heaven below
 My Redeemer to know,
And the angels could do nothing more
 Than to fall at His feet,
 And the story repeat,
And the Lover of sinners adore.

3 Jesus all the day long
 Was my joy and my song :
O that all His salvation may see ;
 He hath loved me, I cried,
 He hath suffered and died,
To redeem even rebels like me.

254. LOOKING UPWARD.

1 COME away to the skies,—
 My beloved, arise,

And rejoice in the day thou wert born ;
 On the festal day,
 Come exulting away,
||: And with singing to Zion return. : ||

2 We have laid up our love,
 With our treasure, above,
Though our bodies continue below;
 The redeemed of the Lord—
 We remember His word,
||: And with singing, to paradise go. : ||

3 For Thy glory we were
 First created, to share
Both Thy nature and kingdom divine ;
 Now created again,
 That our souls may remain,
||: Both in time and eternity, Thine. : ||
C. Wesley.

255. Work, for the Night is Coming.

Miss ANNIE L. WALKER, 1860.

LOWELL MASON, by per.

1. Work, for the night is coming, Work, thro' the morning hours; Work, while the dew is sparkling,

D. S.—*Work, for the night is coming*

Work, 'mid springing flow'rs : Work, when the day grows brighter, Work in the glowing sun ;

When man's work is done.

2 Work, for the night is coming,
 Work through the sunny noon;
Fill brightest hours with labor,
 Rest comes sure and soon.
Give every flying minute
 Something to keep in store:
Work, for the night is coming,
 When man works no more.

3 Work, for the night is coming,
 Under the sunset skies ;
While their bright tints are glowing,
 Work, for daylight flies.
Work till the last beam fadeth,
 Fadeth to shine no more;
Work while the night is darkening,
 When man's work is o'er.

256. Rapture.

C. WESLEY.

English.

1. Oh, how hap-py are they Who their Saviour o - bey, And have laid up their treasures above !

Tongue can never express The sweet comfort and peace Of a soul in its ear - li-est love.

257. Safe in the Arms of Jesus.

FANNY J. CROSBY, 1868.   W. H. DOANE, by per.

1. Safe in the arms of Je - sus, Safe on His gen-tle breast, There by His love o'er - shad-ed,
2. Safe in the arms of Je - sus, Safe from corroding care, Safe from the world's temptations,
3. Je - sus, my heart's dear refuge, Je - sus has died for me; Firm on the Rock of A - ges,

Sweetly my soul shall rest. Hark! 'tis the voice of an - gels, Borne in a song to me,
Sin can-not harm me there. Free from the blight of sor-row, Free from my doubts and fears;
Ev - er my trust shall be. Here let me wait with patience, Wait till the night is o'er;

CHORUS.

O - ver the fields of glo - ry, O - ver the jas-per sea..... Safe in the arms of Je - sus,
On - ly a few more tri - als, On - ly a few more tears!..
Wait till I see the morning Break on the golden shore.

rit.

Safe on His gen-tle breast, There by His love o'er - shad-ed, Sweetly my soul shall rest.

258. So near to the Kingdom.

FANNY J. CROSBY. (PLEADING WITH THEE.) Rev. ROBERT LOWRY

1. So near to the kingdom! yet what dost thou lack? So near to the
2. So near that thou hear-est the songs that re-sound From those who be-
3. O come, or thy sea-son of grace will be past, The door will be
4. To die with no hope! hast thou counted the cost? To die out of

king-dom! what keep-eth thee back? Re-nounce ev-ery i-dol, though
liev-ing, a par-don have found! So near, yet un-will-ing to
closed, and this call be thy last; O where wouldst thou turn if the
Christ, and thy soul to be lost! So near to the king-dom! O

dear it may be, And come to the Sav-iour now pleading with thee.
give up thy sin, When Je-sus is wait-ing to wel-come thee in!
light should de-part That comes from the Spir-it, and shines on thy heart.
come, we im-plore, While Je-sus is pleading, come en-ter the door.

REFRAIN.

Plead - ing with thee, ... The Saviour is pleading, is pleading with thee.

Pleading with thee,   pleading with thee,

Copyright, 1876, by Biglow & Main

155

259. Rescue the Perishing.

FANNY J. CROSBY.   W. H. DOANE, by per.

1. Res - cue the per - ish - ing, Care for the dy - ing, Snatch them in pit - y from
2. Tho' they are slighting Him, Still He is wait - ing, Wait - ing the pen - i - tent
3. Down in the hu - man heart, Crushed by the temp - ter, Feel - ings lie buried that
4. Res - cue the per - ish - ing, Du - ty de - mands it; Strength for thy la - bor the

sin and the grave; Weep o'er the err - ing one, Lift up the fall - en,
child to re - ceive. Plead with them earnest - ly, Plead with them gent - ly:
grace can re - store: Touched by a lov - ing heart, Wak - ened by kind - ness,
Lord will pro - vide: Back to the nar - row way Pa - tient - ly win them;

CHORUS.

Tell them of Je - sus the migh - ty to save. Res - cue the per - ish - ing,
He will for - give if they on - ly be - lieve.
Chords that were brok - en will vi - brate once more.
Tell the poor wanderer a Sav - iour has died.

Care for the dy - ing; Je - sus is mer - ci - ful, Je - sus will save.

260. I was a Wandering Sheep.

Dr. H. Bonar

J. Zundel.

1. I was a wandering sheep, I did not love the fold; I did not love my
2. The Shepherd sought His sheep, The Fa-ther sought His child; They follow'd me o'er
3. No more a wandering sheep, I love to be con-troll'd, I love my ten-der

Shepherd's voice, I would not be con-troll'd; I was a way-ward child, I
vale and hill, O'er des-erts waste and wild: They found me nigh to death, Fam-
Shepherd's voice, I love the peace-ful fold: No more a way-ward child, I

did not love my home, I did not love my Father's voice, I loved a-far to roam.
ish'd, and faint, and lone; They bound me with the bands of love, They sav'd the wandering one.
seek no more to roam, I love my heav'nly Father's voice—I love, I love His home.

261. To-day the Saviour Calls.

Rev. S. F. Smith.

Dr. L. Mason, 1831.

1. To-day the Saviour calls: Ye wand'rers come; O, ye benighted souls, Why longer roam?
2. To-day the Saviour calls: Oh, listen now: Within these sacred walls To Je-sus bow.
3. To-day the Saviour calls: For refuge fly; The storm of justice falls, And death is nigh.
4. The Spirit calls to-day: Yield to His power; Oh, grieve Him not away, 'Tis mercy's hour.

157

262. Jesus Name of Wondrous Love.

ANON.   (ALETTA.)   WM. B. BRADBURY, by per.

1. Je - sus! Name of wondrous love! Name all oth - er names a - bove!
2. Je - sus! Name of price - less worth To the fall - en sons of earth,
3. Je - sus! Name of mer - cy mild, Giv - en to the ho - ly Child,

Un - to which must ev - ery knee Bow in deep hu - mil - i - ty.
For the prom-ise that it gave— "Je - sus shall His peo - ple save."
When the cup of hu - man woe First He tast - ed here be - low. A - men.

Copyrighted 1857, by Wm. B. Bradbury.

4 Jesus! only Name that's given
Under all the mighty heaven,
Whereby man, to sin enslaved,
Bursts his fetters, and is saved.

5 Jesus! Name of wondrous love!
Human name of God above;
Pleading only this we flee,
Helpless, O our God, to Thee.

263. LOVEST THOU ME.

1 HARK! my soul! it is the Lord;
'Tis thy Saviour—hear His word;
Jesus speaks, and speaks to thee,
"Say, poor sinner, lovest thou me?

2 "Can a woman's tender care
Cease towards the child she bare?

Yes, she may forgetful be,
Yet will I remember thee.

3 "Mine is an unchanging love,
Higher than the heights above;
Deeper than the depths beneath—
Free and faithful—strong as death,

4 "Thou shalt see my glory soon,
When the work of grace is done;
Partner of my throne shalt be!
Say, poor sinner! lovest thou me?"

5 Lord! it is my chief complaint,
That my love is weak and faint;
Yet I love Thee, and adore;—
Oh, for grace to love thee more.

Rev. W. Cowper.

264. As with Gladness Men of old.

W. C. DIX.   (DIX.)   CONRAD KOCHER, 1838.

1. As with gladness men of old Did the guiding star be-hold; As with joy they
2 As they of-fered gifts most rare, At that manger rude and bare, So may we with

As with Gladness Men of old.—Concluded.

hailed its light, Leading onward, beaming bright: So, most gracious Lord, may we
ho - ly joy.   Pure and free from sin's al - loy,   All our costliest treasures bring,

Ev - er - more be led to Thee.
Christ! to Thee our heavenly King.   A-men.

3.
Holy Jesus every day
Keep us in the narrow way;
And, when earthly things are past,
Bring our ransomed souls at last
Where they need no star to guide,
Where no clouds Thy glory hide.

265. · **Christian Children**

Rev. J. B. Dykes.

1. We are lit - tle Christian child - ren; Christ, the Son of God Most High,

With His precious blood re-deem'd us. Dy - ing that we might not die.   Amen.

2 We are little Christian children;
  God the Holy Ghost is here,
  Dwelling in our hearts, to make us
  Kind and holy, good and dear.

3 We are little Christian children,
  Saved by Him who loved us most;
  We believe in God Almighty
  Father, Son and Holy Ghost.

159

266. **Come unto Me.**

Mrs. C. H. Esling, 1839.   (HENLEY.)   Lowell Mason, by per.

1. Come un-to me, when shadows dark-ly gath-er, When the sad heart is
2. Large are the man-sions in thy Father's dwelling, Glad are the homes that
3. There, like an E-den blos-som-ing in glad-ness, Bloom the fair flow'rs the

wea-ry and dis-trest, Seek-ing for com-fort from your Heavenly
sor-rows nev-er dim, Sweet are the harps in ho-ly mu-sic
earth too rude-ly press'd; Come un-to me all ye who droop in

Fa-ther, Come un-to me, and I will give you rest.
swell-ing, Soft are the tones which raise the heav-'nly hymn.
sad-ness, Come un-to me, and I will give you rest. A-men.

267. **Take my heart, Oh, Father! take it.**

ANON.   (TALMAR.)   I. B. Woodbury, 1842.

1. Take my heart, O Fa-ther! take it; Make and keep it all Thine own:
2. Fath-er, make me pure and low-ly, Fond of peace and far from strife;

Arr. from Robinson's Spiritual Songs, by per. of the Century Co.

Take my heart.—Concluded.

Let Thy Spir - it   melt and break it— This proud heart of sin   and stone.
Turning from the   paths un - ho - ly   Of this   vain and sin - ful life.

Ever let Thy grace surround me,
　Strengthen me with power divine,
Till Thy cords of love have bound me:
　Make me to be wholly Thine.

May the blood of Jesus heal me,
　And my sins be all forgiven;
Holy spirit take and seal me,
　Guide me in the path to heaven.

268. JESUS CALLS US.

Jesus calls us, o'er the tumult
　Of our life's wild restless sea;
Day by day His sweet voice soundeth,
　Saying, Christian, follow me!

2 Jesus calls us—from the worship
　Of the vain world's golden store;
From each idol that would keep us,—
　Saying, Christian, love me more!

3 In our joys and in our sorrows,
　Days of toil and hours of ease,
Still He calls, in cares and pleasures,—
　Christian, love me more than these!

4 Jesus calls us! by Thy mercies,
　Saviour, may we hear Thy call;
Give our hearts to Thy obedience,
　Serve and love Thee best of all!

Alexander.

269.   One by One the Sands are Flowing.

ADELAIDE A. PROCTER.　　(MT. VERNON.)　　Dr. L. MASON.

1. One by one the sands are flowing, One by one the moments fall: Some are coming,
2. One by one, bright gifts from heaven, Joys are sent thee here be - low; Take them read - i -
3. One by one thy griefs shall meet thee, Do not fear an arm - ed band; One will fade, while

some are going— Do not strive to grasp them all.
ly, when given— Ready, too, to let them go.
oth - ers greet thee, Shadows passing thro' the land.

4 Every hour that fleets so slowly
　Has its task to do or bear;
Luminous the crown, and holy,
　If thou set each gem with care.

5 Hours are golden links—God's tokens,
　Reaching heaven, but one by one
Take them, lest the chain be broken
　Ere thy pilgrimage be done.

Jesus, Saviour! Pass not By.

Mrs. Elizabeth C. Kinney. (COMFORTER.) Thos. Hastings.

1. Je - sus, Sav - iour! pass not by, Lo! we join, as one, to cry,
2. Pros-trate in Thy path we lie, Lest our ve - ry faith should die:
3. Lord, we can - not let Thee go, In Thy church Thy pres - ence show;

"Bless us al - so, pass not by," "Pass not, pass not by!"
Lord, we need Thee, pass not by! "Pass not, pass not by!"
Till Thou bless us we will cry "Pass not, pass not by!"

Lord, ful - fil Thy prom - ise now, Pour Thy bless - ing while we bow;
To Thy gar - ments we will cling, All our need be - fore Thee bring;
Breathe, oh breathe on us, we pray! Here re - new our work to - day,

Turn to us as one, we cry, "Pass not, pass not by!"
Son of Da - vid, hear our cry, "Pass not, pass not by!"
While we wait, and watch, and cry, "Pass not, pass not by!"

271. There is a Happy Land.

ANDREW YOUNG.

Hindostan Air.

I. There is a hap-py land, Far, far a - way, Where saints in glo - ry stand, Bright, bright as day. Oh, how they sweet - ly sing, "Worthy is our Saviour King," Loud let His praises ring, Praise, praise for aye!

2 Come to that happy land,
    Come, come away,
Why will ye doubting stand,
    Why still delay?
Oh, we shall happy be,
When, from sin and sorrow free,
Lord, we shall dwell with Thee,
    Blest, blest for aye.

3 Bright in that happy land,
    Beams every eye:
Kept by a Father's hand,
    Love cannot die.
Oh, then to glory run;
Be a crown and Kingdom won;
And bright, above the sun,
    We'll reign for aye.

272. COMFORTER DIVINE.
Tune—COMFORTER, p. 162.

1 Holy Ghost, the infinite,
    Shine upon our nature's night
    With Thy blessed inward light,
        Comforter Divine!
We are sinful, cleanse us, Lord;
We are faint, Thy strength afford,
Lost, until by Thee restored.
    Comforter Divine!

2 Like the dew, Thy peace distil;
    Guide, subdue our wayward will,
    Things of Christ unfolding still,
        Comforter Divine!
Holy Ghost, the infinite,
    Shine upon our nature's night
    With Thy blessed inward light,
        Comforter divine!

G. Rawson.

163

273.   Hark, the Herald Angels Sing.

C. WESLEY. 1739.   F. B. MENDELSSOHN.

1. Hark! the her - ald an - gels sing, "Glory to the new-born King; Peace on earth, and
2. Hail! the heav'n-born Prince of Peace! Hail! the Sun of righteousness! Light and life to

mer - cy mild; God and sin - ners re - con-ciled;" Joy - ful all ye na - tions rise,
all He brings, Risen with heal-ing in His wings; Let us then with an - gels sing,

Join the tri - umph of the skies; With th'angel - ic host proclaim, Christ is born in
"Glo - ry to the new born King; Peace on earth, and mer - cy mild; God and sin - ners

Beth - le - hem, With th'angel - ic host proclaim, Christ is born in Beth - le - hem.
re - conciled, Peace on earth and mer - cy mild; God and sin - ners re - con - ciled. *Amen.*

274.   Holy Night! Peaceful Night!

M. HAYDN.

1. Ho - ly night! peace - ful night! All is dark, save the light,

Yon - der, where they sweet vi - gil keep O'er the Babe, who, in si - lent sleep,

Rests in hea - ven - ly peace, Rests in hea - ven - ly peace.

2 Holy night! peaceful night!
Only for shepherds' sight,
Came blest visions of Angel throngs,
With their loud Alleluia songs,
  Saying, Jesus is come,
  Saying, Jesus is come.

3 Holy night! peaceful night!
Child of heav'n! O! how bright
Thou didstsmile on us when Thou wast born;
Blest indeed was that happy morn,
  Full of heavenly joy,
  Full of heavenly joy.

275.   CHRIST'S RESURRECTION.

1 CHRIST the Lord is risen to-day!
He Who in the manger lay,
Watch'd by gentle mother's eyes,

Lives and reigns beyond the skies,
"Christ the Lord is risen to-day!"
Each to other gladly say!
Shout, ye happy ones, and sing,
Let the earth with music ring!
Shout, ye happy ones, and sing,
Let the earth with music ring.

2 O the mansions Christ prepares,
Where for each He looks and cares!
O the gardens blooming bright,
Where His glory is the Light!
Here His love is perfect peace,
There His love shall never cease!
Sing, ye children, sing and say,
"Christ the Lord is risen to-day,"
Sing, ye children, sing and say,
"Christ the Lord is risen to-day." *Amen.*

276. The Lord into His Garden comes.

(GARDEN.)

JER. INGALLS, 1805.

1. The Lord in-to His gar-den comes, The spi-ces yield their rich perfumes, The lil-ies grow and thrive; The lil-ies grow and thrive; Re-fresh-ing show'rs of grace di-vine, From Jesus flow to ev-'ry vine, And make the dead re-vive, And make the dead re-vive.

2 Oh, that this dry and barren ground,
In springs of water may abound,—
A fruitful soil become ;
The desert blossoms like the rose,
When Jesus conquers all His foes,
And makes His people one.

3 Come, brethren, you that love the Lord,
Who taste the sweetness of His word,
In Jesus' ways go on ;
Our troubles and our trials here,
Will only make us richer there,
When we arrive at home.

277. RESURRECTION OF CHRIST.

1 COME, see the place where Jesus lay,
And hear angelic watchers say,

"He lives who once was slain !"
Why seek the living 'midst the dead?
Remember how the Saviour said
"That He would rise again."

2 Oh, joyful sound ! oh, glorious hour !
When by His own almighty power
He rose and left the grave !
Now let our songs His triumph tell,
Who burst the bands of death and hell,
And ever lives to save.

3 The first begotten of the dead,
For us He rose, our glorious Head,
Eternal life to bring ;
What tho' the saints like him shall die,
They share their Leader's victory,
And triumph with their King !

Wm. Hammond.

278. Oh, Happy Day.

From E. F. RIMBAULT.

1. { Preserved by Thine Al - mighty power, O Lord, our Mak - er, Saviour, King, }
   { And brought to see this hap-py hour, We come Thy prais - es here to sing. }

CHORUS.

Hap - py day, hap - py day, Here in Thy courts we'll glad-ly stay.

FINE.

D. S.—Hap- py day, hap - py day, When Je - sus washed our sins a - way.

And at Thy foot - stool humbly pray, That Thou wouldst take our sins a - way.

D. S.

2 We praise Thee for Thy constant care,
   For life preserved, for mercies given,
   Oh, may we still those mercies share,
   And taste the joys of sins forgiven.

3 We praise Thee for the joyful news,
   Of pardon through our Saviour's blood:
   O Lord, incline our hearts to choose
   The road to happiness and God.

4 And when on earth our days are done,
   Grant, Lord, that we at length may join
   Teachers and scholars round Thy throne,
   The song of Moses and the Lamb,

279. THE HAPPY CHOICE.

1 Oh, happy day that fixed my choice
   On Thee, my Saviour, and my God!

Well may this glowing heart rejoice,
And tell its raptures all abroad.

CHORUS.—Happy day, happy day,
   When Jesus washed my sins away!
   He taught me how to watch and pray,
   And live rejoicing every day:
   Happy day, happy day,
   When Jesus washed my sins away!

2 Oh happy day, when first we felt
   Our souls with sweet contrition melt,
   And saw our sins, of crimson guilt,
   All cleansed by blood on Calv'ry spilt.

3 Oh happy day, when first Thy love,
   Began our grateful hearts to move;
   And gazing on Thy wond'rous cross,
   We saw all else as worthless dross.—

P. Doddridge.

280. Rest in Jesus' Love.

(ASAPH.)

Dr. L. MASON.

1. All ye that are wea - ry, 'tis Je - sus who calls you, O come to the
2. Come hum-bly to Je - sus, and tell Him your sto - ry Of suffering or

Saviour, and rest in His love, Though dark be the for-tune on earth that be -
sor - row, of guilt or of shame; The par-don of sins is the crown of His

falls you, There's glo - ry e - ter - nal in heav - en a - bove.
glo - ry, The joy of our Lord to be true to His Name.

REFRAIN.

Sweet peace! Rest in His love, Sweet peace! Rest in His love.
Our Lord,— true to His Name, Our Lord,— true to His Name.

281. REST IN HIS LOVE.

1 As DOWN in the sunless retreats of the ocean,
   Sweet flowers are springing no mortal can see;
   So, deep in my heart, the still prayer of devotion,
   Unheard by the world, rises, silent, to Thee,
REFRAIN.—My God, silent to Thee—Pure, warm, silent, to Thee.

2 As still to the star of its worship, though clouded,
   The needle points faithfully o'er the dim sea;
   So, dark as I roam, through this wintry world shrouded,
   The hope of my spirit turns, trembling, to Thee,
REFRAIN.—My God, trembling to Thee—True, fond, trembling, to Thee.

169

282.

God is Love.

JOHN BOWRING.   (WILMOT.)   CARL MARIA VON WEBER.

1. God is love; His mer-cy brightens   All the path in which we rove;
2. Ev'n the hour that dark-est seem-eth,   Will His changeless good-ness prove;
3. He with earth-ly cares en-twin-eth   Hope and com-fort from a-bove;

Bliss He wakes, and woe He light-ens;   God is wis-dom, God is love.
From the gloom His bright-ness streameth,   God is wis-dom, God is love.
Ev-ery-where His glo-ry shin-eth,   God is wis-dom, God is love. Amen.

283.   From the Recesses of a Lowly Spirit.

Chant.

1 FROM the recesses of a lowly spirit,
Our humble prayer ascends, O | Father, | hear it ||
Borne on the trembling wings of | fear and | meekness, ||
For- | give its | weakness. ||

2 We know, we feel how mean, and how un-worthy
The lowly sacrifice we | pour be- | fore Thee: ||
What can we offer Thee, O | Thou most | Holy ! ||
But | sin and folly. ||

3 We see Thy hand, it leads us, it supports us :
We hear Thy voice, it | counsels,..and it | courts us: ||
And then we turn away ! yet | still thy | kindness ||
For- | gives our | blindness. ||

4 Who can resist Thy gentle call, appealing
To every generous thought and | grateful } feeling; ||
Oh'! who can hear the accents | of Thy | mercy. ||
And | never | love Thee. ||

5 Kind Benefactor ! plant within this bosom
The | seeds of | holiness, || and let them blos-som
In fragrance, and in beauty | bright and | vernal, ||
And | spring e- | ternal. ||

6 Then place them in those everlasting gardens
Where angels walk, and | seraphs..are the | wardens; ||
Where every flower, brought safe through } death's dark | portal, ||
Be- | comes im- | mortal. ||

284.　　Beautiful Zion, built Above.

Rev. GEORGE GILL, 1850.　　　　　　　　　　　　　　　　　T. J. COOK.

1. Beau - ti - ful Zi - on, built a - bove, Beau - ti - ful cit - y that I love;
2. Beau - ti - ful heaven, where all is light; Beau - ti - ful an - gels clothed in white;

Beau - ti - ful gates of pearl - y white, Beau - ti - ful tem - ple—God its light.
Beau - ti - ful strains that nev - er tire; Beau - ti - ful harps thro' all the choir—

He who was slain on Cal - va - ry, O-pens those pearl - y gates to me.
There shall I join the chor - us sweet, Worshiping at the Saviour's feet.

REFRAIN.　　　　　　　　　　　　　　　　　　　　　　　Repeat pp.

Zi - on, Zi - on, love - ly Zi - on, Beau - ti - ful Zi - on, cit - y of our God.

3 Beautiful crowns on every brow,
　Beautiful palms the conquerors show:
　Beautiful robes the ransomed wear,
　Beautiful all who enter there—
　Thither I press with eager feet;
　There shall my rest be long and sweet.

4 Beautiful throne for Christ our King,
　Beautiful songs the angels sing;
　Beautiful rest—all wanderings cease;
　Beautiful home of perfect peace—
　There shall my eyes the Saviour see;
　Haste to His heavenly home with me.

A Brighter Day.

THOMAS KELLY.

WM. B. BRADBURY, by per.

1. Yes, we trust the day is break-ing; Joy - ful times are near at hand;
2. While the foe be-comes more dar - ing, While he en - ters like a flood,
3. God of Ja - cob, high and glo - rious, Let Thy peo - ple see Thy hand.

God, the mighty God, is speak-ing By His word in ev - ery land.
God, the Sav - iour, is pre - par - ing Means to spread His truth a - broad.
Let the gos - pel be vic - to - rious Thro' the world, in ev - ery land.

CHORUS.

"Lift your heads," the day is break-ing, Soon the morn-ing will ap - pear;

See the earth from slum-ber wak - ing; "Lift your heads," the day draws near.

Brightest and Best.

Bp. REG. HEBER, 1811.　　　　　(FOLSOM.)　　　JOHANN C. W. MOZART. (1756—1791.)

1. Bright - est and best of the sons of the morn - ing,
2. Cold on His cra - dle the dew - drops are shin - ing,
3. Say, shall we yield Him in cost - ly de - vo - tion,

Dawn on our dark - ness, and lend us Thine aid;
Low lies His head with the beasts of the stall;
O - dors of E - dom, and offer - ings di - vine,

Star of the East, the hor - i - zon a - dorn - ing,
An - gels a - dore Him in slum - ber re - clin - ing,
Gems of the moun - tain, and pearls of the o - cean,

Guide where our in - fant Re - deem - er is laid.
Mak - er, and Mon - arch, and Sav - iour of all.
Myrrh from the for - est, or gold from the mine?　A - men.

4 Vainly we offer each ample oblation;
　Vainly with gifts His favor secure:
Richer by far is the hearts adoration;
　Dearer to God are the prayers of the poor.

5 Brightest and best of the sons of the morning,
　Dawn on our darkness, and lend us Thine aid;
Star of the East, the horizon adorning,
　Guide where our infant Redeemer is laid.

287. Hail to the Brightness.

T. HASTINGS. (WESLEY.) LOWELL MASON.

1. Hail to the brightness of Zi - on's glad morn-ing! Joy to the
2. Hail to the brightness of Zi - on's glad morn-ing, Long by the
3. Lo! in the des - ert rich flow - ers are springing, Streams ev - er
4. See from all lands— from the isles of the o - cean, Praise to Je -

lands that in dark-ness have lain! Hushed be the ac - cents of sor - row and
proph-ets of Is - rael fore - told; Hail to the millions from bondage re -
co - pious are glid - ing a - long; Loud from the mountain-tops ech - oes are
ho - vah as - cend-ing on high; Fall'n are the engines of war and com -

mourning; Zi - on in tri - umph be - gins her mild reign.
turn - ing; Gen - tile and Jew the blest vis - ion be - hold.
ring - ing; Wastes rise in ver - dure, and min - gle in song.
mo - tion, Shouts of sal - va - tion are rend - ing the sky. A - men.

288.

RESURRECTION OF JESUS.

1 HAIL to the brightness which heralds His glory,
    Hail to the coming of Christ among men!
  Back from the tomb He has come, and the story,
    Is told us by angels again and again!

2 Death is uncrowned, since the Saviour of mortals
    The grave and destruction has robbed of their gloom:
  Victory shines out from heav'n's opened portals,
    Jesus has conquered the power of the tomb.

Story of St. John.

173

289. Watchman, Tell Us of the Night.

Sir JOHN BOWRING.　　　　　　　　　　　　　　　　　　　　　　　LOWELL MASON,

1. Watchman, tell us of the night, What its signs of promise are: Traveler, o'er yon mountain's
2. Watchman, tell us of the night, Higher yet that star ascends: Traveler, blessedness and
3. Watchman, tell us of the night, For the morning seems to dawn; Traveler, darkness takes its

height See that glo - ry - beaming star! Watchman, does its beauteous ray Aught of
light, Peace and truth, its course portends, Watchman, will its beams a - lone Gild the
flight, Doubt and ter - ror are withdrawn, Watchman, let thy wanderings cease; Hie thee

joy or hope fore-tell? Trav'ler, yes; it brings the day, Promis'd day of Is - ra - el.
spot that gave them birth? Trav'ler, a - ges are its own, See, it bursts o'er all the earth.
to thy qui - et home; Trav'ler! lo, the Prince of Peace, Lo, the Son of God is come!

May be sung responsively.

CHORUS to 3rd stanza.

Trav'ler! lo, the Prince of Peace. Lo, the Son of God is come! Lo, the Son of God is come!

174

290. That Beautiful Land.

J. HALL.   WM. B. BRADBURY, 1861.

With gentleness.

1. A beau-ti-ful land by faith I see, A land of rest from sor-row free, The
   home of the ran-somed, bright and fair, And beau-ti-ful an-gels, too, are there.

2. That beauti-ful land, the City of Light, It ne'er has known the shades of night; The
   glo-ry of God, the light of day, Hath driv-en the dark-ness far a-way.

CHORUS.

Will you go? Will you go? Go to that beau-ti-ful land with me?

Will you go? Will you go? Go to that beau-ti-ful land?

3 In vision I see its streets of gold,
  Its beautiful gates I, too, behold
  The river of life, the crystal sea,
  The health-giving fruit of life's fair tree.

4 The heavenly throng arrayed in white,
  In rapture range the plains of light;
  And in one harmonious choir they praise
  Their glorious Saviour's matchless grace.

291. Jesus shall Reign where'er the Sun.

I. WATTS. (MISSIONARY CHANT.) H. C. ZEUNER.

1. Je - sus shall reign where'er the sun Does His suc - ces - sive jour - neys run;
2. For Him shall end - less prayer be made, And end - less prais - es crown His head;
3. Peo - ple and realms of ev - ery tongue Dwell on His love, with sweet-est song;

His kingdom stretch from shore to shore, Till moons shall wax and wane no more.
His name, like sweet perfume, shall rise With ev - ery morning sac - ri - fice.
And in - fant voi - ces shall proclaim Their ear-ly blessings on His name. A-men.

4 Blessings abound where'er He reigns;
  The prisoner leaps to lose his chains;
  The weary find eternal rest,
  And all the sons of want are blest.

5 Let every creature rise and bring
  Peculiar honors to our King:
  Angels descend with songs again,
  And earth repeat the loud Amen !

292. My Country 'tis of Thee.

S. F. SMITH, D. D. (AMERICA.) Dr. JOHN BULL.

1. My country! 'tis of thee, Sweet land of lib - er - ty, Of thee I sing: Land where my
2. My na-tive country, thee—Land of the no - ble free—Thy name I love; I love thy

fa - thers died! Land of the Pilgrims' pride! From every mountain side Let freedom ring.
rocks and rills, Thy woods and templed hills; My heart with rapture thrills Like that above. A-men.

My Country 'tis of Thee.—Concluded.

3 Let music swell the breeze,
  And ring from all the trees
    Sweet freedom's song;
  Let mortal tongues awake;
  Let all that breathe partake;
  Let rocks their silence break,—
    The sound prolong.

4 Our father's God! to Thee,
  Author of Liberty,
    To Thee we sing:
  Long may our land be bright
  With freedom's holy light;
  Protect us by Thy might,
    Great God, our King!

293. NATIONAL SONG.

1 God bless our native land!
  Firm may she ever stand,
    Through storm and night;
  When the wild tempests rave,
  Ruler of wind and wave,
  Do Thou our country save
    By Thy great might.

2 For her our prayer shall rise
  To God, above the skies;
    On Him we wait:
  Thou who art ever nigh,
  Guarding with watchful eye,
  To Thee aloud we cry,
    God save the State.

Dr. Leonard Bacon.

294.   The Prince of Salvation.

1. Now the new Cre-a-tion Is in Thee be-gun, All that Adam lost us More than won.

2. Thou art the Incarnate, God with man made one, Giving man once more the Place of Son. Amen.

3 Thou art born to free us
  From the power of earth,
  Bringing us to Thee in
    The New Birth.

4 Thou art born to save us
  From the power of sin,
  From the evil round us
    And within.

5 Thou art born to change us
  By Thy grace Divine,
  And to make our natures
    Like to Thine.

6 Thou hast left Thy glory,
  Far beyond the skies,
  That with Thee to heaven
    We may rise.

7 One with Thee, O Saviour,
  May our lives be blest,
  One with Thee O bring us
    To Thy rest.

8 While by faith we see Thee,
  May our hearts adore,
  Till our eyes behold Thee
    Ever more.

295. The Solid Rock.

Rev. EDWARD MOTE, 1825.   WM. B. BRADBURY, by per.

1. My hope is built on noth-ing less Than Je-sus' blood and
2. When dark-ness veils His love-ly face, I rest on His un-
3. When he shall come with trum-pet sound, O, may I then in

righteous-ness; I dare not trust the sweetest frame, But whol-ly lean on
changing grace; In ev-ery high and storm-y gale, My an-chor holds with-
Him be found; Drest in His right-eous-ness a-lone, Fault-less to stand be-

CHORUS.

Je-sus' name. On Christ, the Sol-id Rock, I stand; All
in the vail.
fore the throne.

oth-er ground is sink-ing sand, All oth-er ground is sink-ing sand.

296. My Days are Gliding swiftly By.

D. NELSON. (SHINING SHORE.) GEO. F. ROOT, by per.

1. My days are glid-ing swift-ly by, And I, a pil-grim stran-ger,
2. We'll gird our loins, my breth-ren dear, Our heavenly home dis-cern-ing;

Would not de-tain them as they fly, Those hours of toil and dan-ger.
Our ab-sent Lord has left us word, Let ev-ery lamp be burn-ing.

REFRAIN.

For, oh. we stand on Jor-dan's strand, Our friends are pass-ing o-ver;

And, just be-fore, the Shin-ing Shore We may al-most dis-cov-er !

3 Should coming days be cold and dark,
    We need not cease our singing;
  That perfect rest naught can molest,
    Where golden harps are ringing.—REF.

4 Let sorrow's rudest tempest blow,
    Each cord on earth to sever;
  Our King says, "Come," and there's our home
    For ever, oh, for ever !—REF.

297. The King of Love my Shepherd is.

HENRY W. BAKER. (DOMINUS REGIT ME.)

Joyful.

1. The King of love my Shepherd is, Whose goodness faileth nev - er; I nothing lack if
2. Where streams of living wa - ter flow My ransom'd soul He lead-eth, And, where the verdant
3. Perverse and foolish, oft I stray'd, But yet in love He sought me, And on His shoulder

I am His, And He is mine for ev - er.
pastures grow, With food ce-lest-ial feedeth.
gent-ly laid, And home, rejoicing brought me. *Amen.*

4 In death's dark vale I fear no ill
  With Thee, dear Lord, beside me;
Thy rod and staff my comfort still,
  Thy Cross before to guide me.

5 And so, through all the length of days,
  Thy goodness faileth never;
Good Shepherd, may I sing Thy praise
  Within Thy house forever!

298. Jesus, tender Shepherd, hear me.

Mrs. MARY LUNDIE DUNCAN. (ST. SYLVESTER.) The Rev. JOHN B. DYKES, 1861.

1. Je - sus, ten-der Shepherd, hear me; Bless Thy lit - tle lamb to - night:
2. All this day Thy hand has led me, And I thank Thee for Thy care;
3. Let my sins be all for - giv - en, Bless the friends I love so well;

Thro' the darkness be Thou near me, Keep me safe till morning light.
Thou hast clothed me, warmed and fed me, List - en to my evening prayer.
Take me when I die to heav - en, Hap - py there with Thee to dwell. A - men.

180

299.

Jesus, Blessed Mediator!

Rev. J. Conder.

(GUIDANCE.)

Fred. von Flotow, arr. by H. P. Main.

1. Je - sus, blessed Me - di - a - tor! Thou the air - y path hast trod; Thou the Judge, the
2. Blessed fold! no foe can en - ter; And no friend de-part-eth thence; Je - sus is their

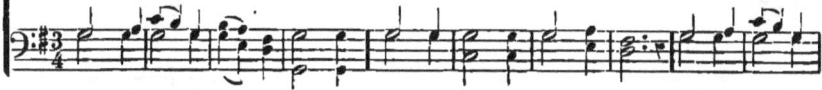

Con-sum - ma - tor! Shepherd of the fold of God! Can I trust a fel - low-
sun, their cen - ter, And their shield, Om-ni - po - tence. Blessed! for the Lamb shall

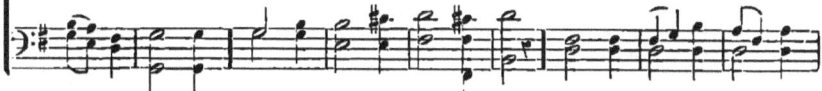

be - ing? Can I trust an an - gel's care? O Thou mer-ci - ful All - see - ing!
feed them, All their tears shall wipe a - way, To the liv - ing fountains lead them,

Beam a-round my spir - it there, Beam a - round my spir-it there.
Till fru - i - tion's per - fect day, Till fru - i - tion's perfect day. A - men.

181

300.   Onward, Christian Soldiers.

S. BARING-GOULD.

(ST. GERTRUDE.)

A. S. SULLIVAN.

1. Onward, Christian sol-diers, Marching as to war; With the cross of Je - sus,
2. Like a might-y arm - y, Moves the Church of God; Brothers, we are tread - ing

Go - ing on be - fore. Christ, the roy - al Mas - ter, Leads a - gainst the foe;
Where the saints have trod; We are not di - vid - ed, All one bod - y we,

CHORUS.

Forward in - to bat - tle, See, His banners go. On-ward, Christian sol - diers,
One in hope and doc - trine, One in char - i - ty.

Marching as to war, With the cross of Je - sus, Go - ing on be - fore. A - men.
war, With the cross of Je - sus,

3 Crowns and thrones may perish,
Kingdoms rise and wane,
But the Church of Jesus
Constant will remain;
Gates of hell can never
'Gainst that Church prevail;
We have Christ's own promise,
And that cannot fail.—CHO.

4 Onward, then, ye people,
Join our happy throng;
Blend with ours your voices
In the triumph-song;
Glory, laud, and honor,
Unto Christ the King;
This through countless ages,
Men and angels sing.—CHO.

301. Brightly Gleams our Banner.

T. J. POTTER.　　　　　　　(ST. ALBANS.)　　　　　From F. J. HAYDN.

1. Brightly gleams our banner, Pointing to the sky, Wav-ing wand'rers on-ward
2. Je - sus, Lord and Master, At Thy sa - cred feet, Here with hearts re - joic - ing
3. All our days di - rect us In the way we go; Lead us on vic - to - rious

To their homes on high, Journeying o'er the des-ert, Glad-ly thus we pray,
See Thy chil - dren meet; Oft - en we have left Thee, Oft - en gone a - stray;
O - ver ev - ery foe: Bid Thine an - gels shield us When the storm-clouds lower,

REFRAIN.

And with hearts u - nit - ed Take our heavenward way. Brightly gleams our ban-ner
Keep us, might - y Sav-iour In the nar - row way.
Par - don Thou and save us In the last dread hour.

Pointing to the sky, Wav-ing wand'rers on-ward To their homes on high.

188

302. Come thou Fount of every Blessing.

ROBERT ROBINSON, 1758.   (AUTUMN.)   Spanish: From MARECHIO.

1. Come, thou Fount of ev - ery bless-ing, Tune my heart to sing Thy grace;
2. Oh, to grace how great a debt - or Dai - ly I'm constrained to be!

Streams of mer - cy, nev - er ceas - ing, Call for songs of loud - est praise;
Let Thy good-ness, like a fet - ter, Bind my wandering heart to Thee;

Teach me some me - lo - dious son - net, Sung by flam - ing tongues a - bove:
Prone to wan - der, Lord, I feel it; Prone to leave the God I love;

Praise the mount—I'm fixed up - on it! Mount of Thy re-deem - ing love.
Here's my heart; oh, take and seal it; Seal it for Thy courts a - bove.

303. Jesus, I my Cross have taken.

HENRY FRANCIS LYTE, 1825.   arr. by H. P. MAIN, 1878.

1. Je - sus, I my cross have tak - en, All to leave and fol - low Thee;

Nak - ed, poor, des - pised, for - sak - en, Thou, from hence, my all shalt be!

Per - ish ev - ery fond am - bi - tion, All I've sought, or hoped, or known;

Yet how rich is my con - di - tion, God and heaven are still my own!

2 Let the world despise and leave me;
   They have left my Saviour, too;
Human hearts and looks deceive me;
   Thou art not, like man, untrue;
And, while Thou shalt smile upon me,
   God of wisdom, love, and might!
Foes may hate, and friends may shun me;
   Show Thy face, and all is bright.

3 Man may trouble and distress me;
   'Twill but drive me to Thy breast;
Life with trials hard may press me,
   Heaven will bring me sweeter rest:
Oh! 'tis not in grief to harm me,
   While Thy love is left to me;
Oh! 'twere not in joy to charm me,
   Were that joy unmixed with Thee.

304. **Jesus, on His glorious Throne.**

J. NEWTON. (MELODY.) A. CHAPIN.

1. Je-sus, who on His glorious throne Rules heaven, and earth, and sea, Is pleased to claim me
2. His per-son fix - es all my love, His blood removes my fear; And while He pleads for

for His own And give himself to me.
me a 'bove, His arm preserves me here. *Amen.*

3 His word of promise is my food,
  His Spirit is my guide;
  Thus daily is my strength renewed,
  And all my wants supplied.

4 For Him I count as gain each loss,
  Disgrace for Him renown;
  Well may I glory in my cross,
  While He prepares my crown.

305. JESUS, OUR LORD.

1 I'M not ashamed to own my Lord,
  Or to defend His cause;
  Maintain the honor of His word,
  The glory of His cross.

2 Jesus, my God!—I know His name—
  His name is all my trust;
  Nor will He put my soul to shame,
  Nor let my hope be lost.

3 Firm as His throne, His promise stands,
  And He can well secure
  What I've committed to His hands,
  Till the decisive hour.

4 Then will He own my worthless name,
  Before His Father's face,
  And in the new Jerusalem
  Appoint my soul a place.

Isaac Watts.

306. **Immanuel's Banner.**

REV. THERON BROWN. REV. GEO. G. PHIPPS.

Spirited.

1. The Banner of Im-man-u-el! Beneath its glorious folds For life or death to
2. The bat-tles of a thousand years, Its sa-cred col-ors stain; The sto-ry of His
3. "Sal-va-tion by the blood of Christ!" The shouts of triumph ring, No oth-er watchword

serve and fight, We pledge our loy-al souls, No oth-er flag such hon-or boasts, Or
vic - to - ries, Who died and lives a - gain, And still as bright its wing of light, The
leads the host That serves the grandest King. Then ral - ly, sol - diers of the cross! Keep

Copyright, 1884, by Rev. F. N. Palmbut.

188

Immanuel's Banner.—Concluded.

bears so proud a name, And far its red - cross sig - nal
morn - ing winds un - roll, And still its glo - ries sweep the
ev - ery fold un - furled, And Thy re - demp - tion's ho - ly

flies, And far its red - cross sig - nal flies, As flies the lightning's flame.
sky, And still its glo - ries sweep the sky, And flash from pole to pole.
sign, And Thy re - demp - tion's ho - ly sign, Will con - quer all the world.

307. How precious is the Book Divine.

J. FAWCETT. (KNOX.)

1. How precious is the book divine, By in - spi - ra - tion given, Bright as a lamp - its
2. O'er all the strait and narrow way Its radiant beams are cast; A light whose nev - er

doctrines shine, To guide our souls to heaven.
wea - ry ray Grows brightest at the last.

3 It sweetly cheers our drooping hearts,
   In this dark vale of tears;
   Life, light, and joy it still imparts,
   And quells our rising fears.

4 This lamp, through all the tedious night
   Of life, shall guide our way,
   Till we behold the clearer light
   Of an eternal day.

308. There is an Hour of Peaceful Rest.

W. B. Tappan.　　　　　(WOODLAND.)　　　　　N. D. Gould.

1. There is　an hour　of peace - ful rest,　To mourning wand'rers giv'n;
2. There is　a home　for wea - ry souls,　By sin and sorrow driv'n,—

There is　a joy　for souls distressed　A balm for ev - ery
When tossed on　life's tem - pest - uous shoals,　Where storms a - rise, and

wound - ed breast;　'Tis found　a - bove— in heaven.
o - cean rolls,　And all　is drear— but heaven. A - men.

3 There faith lifts up her cheerful eye
　To brighter prospects given;
　And views the tempest passing by,
　The evening shadows quickly fly,
　And all serene—in heaven.

4 There fragrant flowers immortal bloom,
　And joys supreme are given ;
　There rays divine disperse the gloom;
　Beyond the confines of the tomb
　Appears the dawn of heaven !

309. THE EVER-LIVING SOUL.

1 Sweet day ! so cool, so calm, so bright,
　Bridal of earth and sky;

The dew shall weep thy fall to-night,
　For thou, alas ! must die.

2 Sweet rose ! in air whose odors wave,
　And colors charm the eye;
　Thy root is ever in the grave,
　And thou, alas ! must die.

3 Sweet spring ! of days and roses made,
　Whose charms for beauty vie,
　Thy days depart, thy roses fade,
　Thou, too, alas ! must die.

4 Only a sweet and holy soul
　Hath tints that never fly;
　While flowers decay, and seasons roll,
　It lives, and cannot die.
　　　　　　　　　　　　Herbert.

188

310.   Sound the Battle Cry!

WM. F. SHERWIN.   WM. F. SHERWIN, by per.

Vigorously, in march time.

1. Sound the bat - tle cry! See! the foe is nigh; Raise the standard high For the Lord;
2. Strong to meet the foe, Marching on we go, While our cause we know Must pre - vail;
3. Oh! Thou God of all, Hear us when we call; Help us one and all By Thy grace;

Gird your ar - mor on, Stand firm ev - ery one; Rest your cause upon His ho - ly word.
Shield and banner bright Gleaming in the light; Battling for the right We ne'er can fail.
When the battle's done, And the vict-'ry won, May we wear the crown Be - fore Thy face.

CHORUS. *ff*

Rouse then soldiers! ral - ly round the banner! Read-y, stead-y, pass the word a - long;

On-ward, for-ward, shout aloud Hosan - na! Christ is Captain of the mighty throng.

311. Blessed are the Sons of God.

J. HUMPHREYS. (ROSEFIELD.) Dr. C. H. A. MALAN.

1. { Blessed are the sons of God, They are bought with Christ's own blood }
   { They are ransomed from the grave; Life e - ter - nal they shall have: } With them numbered

2. { They are jus - ti-fied by grace, They en-joy the Saviour's peace; }
   { All their sins are washed away; They shall stand in God's great day: } With them, &c.

may we be, Here, and in e - ter - ni - ty. Amen.

3 They are lights upon the earth,
  Children of a heavenly birth,—
  One with God, with Jesus one:
  Glory is in them begun:
  With them numbered may we be,
  Here, and in eternity.

312. We give Thee but Thine Own.

(EVENING.) A. CHAPIN.

1. We give Thee but Thine own, What-e'er the gift may be; All that we have is
2. May we Thy boun-ties thus As stew-ards true re-ceive, And glad-ly, as Thou
3. To comfort and to bless, To find a balm for woe, To tend the lone and

Thine a - lone, A trust, O Lord, from Thee.
bless-est us, To Thee our first fruits give.
fa - ther-less Is an - gel's work be - low.

4 The captive to release,
  To God the lost to bring,
  To teach the way of life and peace,
  It is a Christ-like thing.

5 And we believe Thy word,
  Though dim our faith may be;
  Whate'er for Thine we do, O Lord,
  We do it unto Thee.

313. I'm a Pilgrim.

Mrs. M. S. B. DANA, 1841.

"BUONA NOTTE," Italian Melody.

1. I'm a pil-grim, and I'm a stranger: I can tar-ry, I can tar-ry but a night.
2. There the sunbeams are ev-er shin-ing, Oh, my longing heart, my longing heart is there;
3. Of that country, to which I'm go-ing, My Re-deemer, my Redeem-er is the light:

Do not de-tain me, for I am go-ing To where the streamlets are ev-er flowing,
Here in this country, so dark and drea-ry. I long have wandered forlorn and wea-ry:
There is no sor-row, nor a-ny sighing, Nor a-ny sin there, nor a-ny dy-ing.

CHORUS.

I'm a pil-grim, and I'm a stranger: I can tar-ry, I can tar-ry but a night.

314. Tune—EVENING.

1 THE day is past and gone,
The evening shades appear!
Oh! may we all remember well
The night of death draws near.

2 We lay our garments by,
Upon our beds to rest;
So death will soon disrobe us all
Of what we here possessed.

3 Lord, keep us safe this night,
Secure from all our fears;

May angels guard us while we sleep,
Till morning light appears.

4 And when we early rise,
And view the unwearied sun,
May we set out to win the prize,
And after glory run.

5 And when our days are past,
And we from time remove,
Oh, may we in Thy bosom rest,
The bosom of Thy love!

191

315.
Come, Holy Spirit, Heavenly Dove.
(STEPHENS.)

I. WATTS.   WM. JONES.

1. Come, Ho - ly Spir - it, heaven - ly Dove! With all Thy quickening powers,
2. Look! how we grov - el here be - low, Fond of these tri - fling toys!
3. In vain we tune our for - mal songs; In vain we strive to rise;

Kin - dle a flame of sa - cred love In these cold hearts of ours.
Our souls can nei - ther fly nor go To reach e - ter - nal joys.
Ho - san - nas lan - guish on our tongues, And our de - vo - tion dies.

4 Dear Lord, and shall we ever live
  At this poor dying rate—
Our love so faint, so cold to Thee,
  And Thine to us so great?

5 Come, Holy Spirit, heavenly Dove!
  With all Thy quickening powers;
Come, shed abroad a Saviour's love,
  And that shall kindle ours.

316.
Come, Holy Spirit.
(TURNER.)

A. MAXIM.

1. Come, Ho - ly Spir - it, Heavenly Dove, With all Thy quick'ning pow'rs;   Kin -

Kin-dle a flame of

dle a flame of sa - cred love, Kin - dle a flame of sa - cred love. In these cold

Kin - dle a flame of sa - cred love In these cold

sa - - - cred love In these cold hearts of ours, In

Come, Holy Spirit.—Concluded.

these cold hearts of ours, Kin-dle a flame of sa-cred love In these cold hearts of ours.

these cold hearts of ours.

317. Just as I am, without one Plea.

Miss C. ELLIOTT.　　　(WOODWORTH.)　　　WM. B. BRADBURY.

1. Just as I am, with-out one plea, But that Thy blood was shed for me,
2. Just as I am, and waiting not To rid my soul of one dark blot,
3. Just as I am, tho' tossed about With many a con-flict, many a doubt,

And that Thou bid'st me come to Thee, O Lamb of God, I come! I come!
To Thee whose blood can cleanse each spot, O Lamb of God, I come! I come!
Fightings and fears, with-in, with-out, O Lamb of God, I come! I come!

4 Just as I am—Thou wilt receive,
　Wilt welcome, pardon, cleanse, relieve;
　Because Thy promise I believe,
　　O Lamb of God, I come!

5 Just as I am—Thy love unknown
　Hath broken every barrier down;
　Now, to be Thine, yea, Thine alone,
　　O Lamb of God, I come!

318. O, PRECIOUS SAVIOUR.

1 O PRECIOUS Saviour, who on earth
　For children stooped to mortal birth,
　That we, from every sin set free,
　Children of God might truly be.

2 Thou Light, sent forth from God's own hand,
　Into our darkling earthly land,
　A child of heaven, a heavenly glow,
　To draw our souls from shades below.

3 Dear Saviour! bless a little child,
　And make my spirit pure and mild,
　O cleanse my soul from heaven above
　In the rich fountains of Thy love.

4 That I may like God's angels be,
　In Love and in Humility,—
　With Thee the crown of joy to wear;
　This, blessed Jesus, is my prayer!

319.

Salvation! O the Joyful Sound.

ISAAC WATTS   (CAMBRIDGE.)   JOHN RANDALL.

1. Sal - va - tion! O the joy - ful sound! What pleas - ure to our ears!
2. Sal - va - tion! let the ech - o fly The spa - cious earth a - round,
3. Sal - va - tion! O Thou bleed - ing Lamb! To Thee the praise be - longs:

A sovereign balm for ev - ery wound, A cor - dial for our
While all the ar - mies of the sky Con - spire to raise the
Sal - va - tion shall in - spire our hearts, And dwell up - on our

fears, A cor - dial for our fears, A cor - dial for our fears.
sound, Con - spire to raise the sound, Con - spire to raise the sound.
tongues, And dwell up - on our tongues, And dwell up - on our tongues.

320.

Thy Will be done.

J. BOWRING.   FINE.   LOWELL MASON, 1840.

1. "Thy will be | done!" || In devious way The... | | || Yet still our grateful... | |
        hurrying stream of | life may | run ; || hearts shall say, | "Thy will be | done!"
2. "Thy will be ! done!" || If o'er us shine A glad- | | || This prayer will make it | |
        dening and a | prosperous | sun, || more divine— | "Thy will be | done!"
3. "Thy will be ! done!" || Tho' shrouded o'er Our | path with | gloom,|| one comfort—one is ours:— | |
        to breathe, while we adore, | "Thy will be | done!"

321.

Avison.

WM. A. MUHLENBERG, D. D.

CHARLES AVIS

[V. 1 & 2] V. 3. ✱

CHORUS.

Shout the glad tidings, ex-ult-ing-ly sing; Je - ru - sa-lem triumphs, Messiah is King! King.

1. Zi - on, the mar-vel-lous sto - ry be tell-ing, The Son of the Highest, how
2. Tell how He com-eth, from na - tion to na - tion, The heart-cheering news let the
3. Mor-tals, your hom-age be grate-ful - ly bringing, And sweet let the gladsome ho-

low - ly His birth, The brightest arch-an - gel in glo - ry ex - cell-ing, He
earth ech - o round, How free to the faith-ful He of - fers sal - va - tion,— His
san - na a - rise; Ye an - gels, the full hal - le - lu - jah be sing-ing, One

rit.

D. C. for CHORUS. | ✱ After 3rd verse, let Chorus end with this line.

stoops to re-deem thee, He reigns up - on earth. Mes-si - ah is King, Mes-si-ah is King!
peo - ple with joy ev - er - last - ing are crowned.
cho - rus resound thro' the earth and the skies.

322. Crusader's Hymn.

Unknown 12th Century.

1. Fair-est Lord Je - sus, Ru - ler of all na - ture, O Thou of God and man the Son!
2. Fair are the meadows, Fair-er still the woodlands, Robed in the blooming garb of spring;
3. Fair is the sunshine, Fair-er still the moonlight, And all the twinkling, star-ry host;

Thee will I cher-ish, Thee will I hon - or, Thou, my soul's glo - ry, joy and crown.
Je - sus is fair - er, Je - sus is pur - er, Who makes the woe-ful heart to sing.
Je - sus shines brighter, Je - sus shines pur-er, Than all the an-gels heaven can boast.

323. Jesus, my all.

FANNY J. CROSBY, 1865.   ARR. by T. E. PERKINS.

1. Lord, at Thy mercy-seat. Humbly I fall; Pleading Thy promise sweet, Lord, hear my call;
2. Tears of repentant grief Si - lent - ly fall; Help Thou my un-be-lief, Hear Thou my call.
3. Hark! how the words of love Tender - ly fall, Ere to the realms above, Heard is my call;
4. Still at Thy mercy-seat Humbly I fall; Pleading Thy promise sweet, Heard is my call.

Now let Thy work begin, Oh, make me pure within, Cleanse me from every sin, Jesus my all.
Oh, how I pine for Thee! 'Tis all my hope, and plea: Jesus has died for me, Je - sus, my all.
Now every doubt has flown, Broken my heart of stone, Lord, I am Thine alone, Jesus my all.
Faith wings my soul to Thee: This all my hope shall be, Jesus has died for me, Jesus, my all.

324. The Golden Shore.

Rev. CHARLES DUNBAR, 1858. WM. B. BRADBURY (1816—1868), 1859.

1. We are out on the o-cean sailing, Homeward bound we swiftly glide; We are out on the
2. Millions now are safe-ly land-ed, O-ver on the golden shore: Millions more are

CHORUS. *Cres.*

o - cean sail-ing, To a home be-yond the tide. All the storms will soon be o - ver,
on their journey, Yet there's room for millions more.

Then we'll an - chor in the harbor, We are out on the o - cean sail-ing, To a home be -

yond the tide, We are out on the o-cean sail-ing To a home beyond the tide.

325. Come, ye Disconsolate.

T. MOORE.   S. WEBBE.

1. Come, ye dis - con - so - late, where - e'er ye lan - guish; Come to the
2. Joy of the com - fort - less, light of the stray - ing, Hope of the
3. Here see the Bread of Life; see wa - ters flow - ing Forth from the

mer - cy - seat, fer - vent - ly kneel; Here bring your wounded hearts,
pen - i - tent, fade - less and pure; Here speaks the Com - for - ter
throne of God, pure from a - bove; Come to the feast of love:

here tell your anguish, Earth has no sor - row that heaven can - not heal.
ten - der - ly say - ing— Earth has no sor - row that heaven can - not cure.
come, ev - er knowing Earth has no sor - row but heaven can re - move.

326. Thou dear Redeemer, dying Lamb.

JOHN CENNICK.   (RHINE.)   Arr. fr. FREDERICK BURGMÜLLER.

1. Thou dear Redeemer, dy - ing Lamb, I love to hear of Thee; No music's like Thy
2. O let me ev - er hear Thy voice In mer - cy to me speak; In Thee, my Priest, will
3. My Je - sus shall be still my theme, While in this world I stay; I'll sing my Je - sus'
4. When I appear in yonder cloud, With all Thy favored throng, Then will I sing more

Thou dear Redeemer.—Concluded.

charming name, Nor half so sweet can be, Nor half so sweet can be.
I re-joice, And Thy sal-va-tion seek, And Thy sal-va-tion seek.
love-ly name When all things else de-cay, When all things else de-cay,
sweet, more loud, And Christ shall be my song, And Christ shall be my song.

327.

1 O MOTHER dear, Jerusalem,
　When shall I come to Thee?
When shall my sorrows have an end?
　Thy joys when shall I see?

2 O happy harbor of God's saints!
　O sweet and pleasant soil!
In Thee no sorrow can be found,
　Nor grief, nor care, nor toil.

3 No dimly cloud o'ershadows Thee,
　Nor gloom, nor darksome night;
But every soul shines as the sun,
　For God himself gives light.

4 Thy walls are made of precious stone
　Thy bulwarks diamond-square,
Thy gates are all of orient pearl—
　O God! if I were there!

D. Dickson.

328.　　　O Holy Saviour! Friend unseen.

C. ELLIOTT.　　　　　　(FLEMMING.)　　　　　F. F. FLEMMING.

1. O Ho-ly Saviour! Friend un-seen, Since on Thine arm Thou bid'st me
2. What tho' the world de-ceit-ful prove, And earth-ly friends and hopes re-

lean, Help me, throughout life's changing scene. By faith to cling to Thee.
move; With patient, un-com-plain-ing love, Still would I cling to Thee.

3 Though oft I seem to tread alone
　Life's dreary waste, with thorns o'ergrown,
Thy voice of love, in gentlest tone,
　Still whispers, "Cling to me!"

4 Though faith and hope are often tried,
　I ask not, need not, aught beside;
So safe, so calm, so satisfied,
　The soul that clings to Thee!

329   Mine Eyes have seen the Glory.

MRS. JULIA WARD HOWE.

1. Mine eyes have seen the glo - ry of the com-ing of the Lord; He is tramping
2. He has sounded forth the trumpet that shall nev-er call re - treat; He is sift - ing
3. In the beau-ty of the lil - ies Christ was born a - cross the sea, With a glo - ry

out the vint - age where the grapes of wrath were stored; He hath loosed the fate - ful
out the hearts of men be - fore His judgment-seat; Oh, be swift, my soul, to.
in His bo - som that trans - fig - ures you and me; As He died to make men

CHORUS.

lightning of His terrible quick sword; His truth is marching on.   Glo - ry, glory, hal-le -
an-swer Him! be ju-bi - lant, my feet; Our God is marching on.
ho - ly, let us die to make men free, While God is marching on.

lu-jah! Glory, glory, hal-le - lu - jah! Glory, glo-ry, hal-le - lu-jah! His truth is marching on.

330. **Give me the Wings of Faith.**

Rev I. Watts, 1709.

Arr. by Walter Kittredge.

Solo.

1. Give me the wings of faith to rise, With - in the vail, and see The
2. Once they were mourners here be - low, And pour'd out cries and tears; They
3. I ask them whence their victory came: They, with u - nit - ed breath, As -

saints a - bove, how great their joys, How bright their glo - ries be.
wres - tled hard, as we do now, With sins, and doubts, and fears.
cribe their con - quest to the Lamb, Their tri - umph to His death.

Chorus.

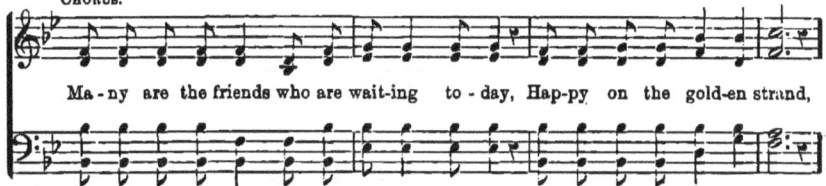

Ma - ny are the friends who are wait - ing to - day, Hap - py on the gold - en strand,

Ma - ny are the voic - es call - ing us a - way, To join their glo - rious band.

Repeat pp.

Call - ing us a - way, Call - ing us a - way, Call - ing to the bet - ter land.

331. Some Sweet Day, By and By.

EDNA L. PARK.

W. H. DOANE, by per.

Tenderly.

1. We shall reach the summer land, Some sweet day, by and by; We shall press the golden
2. At the crys-tal river's brink, Some sweet day, by and by; We shall find each broken
3. O these parting scenes will end, Some sweet day, by and by: We shall gather friend with

strand, Some sweet day, by and by; O the loved ones watching there, By the tree of life so
link, Some sweet day, by and by; Then the star that, fading here, Left our hearts and homes so
friend, Some sweet day, by and by; There before our Father's throne, When the mists and clouds have

REFRAIN.

fair, Till we come their joy to share, Some sweet day, by and by. By and
drear, We shall see more bright and clear, Some sweet day, by and by.
flown, We shall know as we are known, Some sweet day, by and by. By and by, yes,

by, Some sweet day, We shall meet our loved ones gone, Some sweet day, by and by,
by and by,

332. Must Jesus bear the Cross alone?

T. SHEPHERD, alt. (MAITLAND.) GEORGE N. ALLEN, 1849.

1. Must Je-sus bear the cross a - lone, And all the world go free? No, there's a cross for
2. How happy are the saints a-bove, Who once went sorrowing here! But now they taste un -
3. The con-se-crated cross I'll bear, Till death shall set me free; And then go home my

ev - ery one, And there's a cross for me.
mingled love, And joy without a tear.
crown to wear, And there's a crown for me.

4 Upon the crystal pavement, down
    At Jesus' pierced feet,
Joyful, I'll cast my golden crown,
    And His dear name repeat.

5 Oh, precious cross! oh, glorious crown!
    Oh, resurrection day!
Ye angels, from the stars come down,
    And bear my soul away.

333. A Glory gilds the Sacred Page.

(LANESBORO.) WM. DIXON, 1790.

1. A glo-ry gilds the sa-cred page, Ma-jes-tic, like the sun; It gives a light to
2. The hand that gave it, still sup-plies The gracious light and heat; Its truths up-on the
3. Let ev-er-last-ing thanks be Thine, For such a bright dis-play, As makes a world of

ev - ery age; It gives a light to ev-ery age; It gives, but bor-rows none.
na-tions rise,—Its truths up - on the na-tions rise,—They rise, but nev-er set.
darkness shine, As makes a world of dark-ness shine With beams of heavenly day.

There's a Green Hill far away.

Mrs. CECIL FRANCES ALEXANDER

RICHARD STORRS WILLIS, 1860.

1. There is a green hill far a - way, With - out a cit - y wall,
2. He died that we might be for-given, He died to make us good,
3. O dear - ly, dear - ly has He loved, And we must love Him too,

Where the dear Lord was cru - ci - fied, Who died to save us all.
That we might go at last to heaven Saved by His pre - cious blood.
And trust in His re - deem - ing blood, And try His works to do.

We may not know, we can - not tell, What pain He had to bear,
There was no oth - er, good e - nough To pay the price of sin;
For there's a green hill far a - way, With - out a cit - y wall,

But we be - lieve it was for us He hung and suffered there.
He on - ly, could un - lock the gate Of heaven, and let us in.
Where the dear Lord was cru - ci - fied, Who died to save us all. A-men.

335. In the Christian's Home in Glory.

SAMUEL YOUNG HARMER, 1856.

Rev. WILLIAM McDONALD. 1856.

1. In the Christian's home in glo - ry, There re - mains a land of rest;
2. Pain and sick - ness ne'er shall en - ter, Grief nor woe my lot shall share;
3. Sing, oh sing, ye heirs of glo - ry, Shout your tri - umph as you go;

There my Sav-iour's gone be - fore me, To ful - fil my soul's re - quest.
But, in that ce - les - tial cen - tre, I a crown of life shall wear.
Zi - on's gate will o - pen for you, You shall find an en - trance through.

CHORUS.

There is rest for the wea - ry, There is rest for the wea - ry,
On the oth - er side of Jor - dan, In the sweet fields of E - den,

There is rest for the wea - ry, There is rest for you.
Where the tree of life is bloom - ing There is rest for you.

336. O Paradise!

Rev. F. W. Faber, 1862.

Joseph Barnby

1. O Par - a - dise! O Par - a - dise! Who doth not crave for rest?
2. O Par - a - dise! O Par - a - dise! We're look - ing, wait - ing here;

Who would not seek the hap - py land Where they that loved, are blest?
We long to be where Je - sus is, To feel, and see Him near.

Cho.—Where loy - al hearts and true

Where loy - al hearts and true Stand ev - er in the light,

For last verse.

All rap - ture through and through, In God's most ho - ly sight. A - men.

3 O Paradise! O Paradise!
    We want to sin no more,
    We want to be as pure on earth
    As on Thy spotless shore.

4 Lord Jesus, Prince of Paradise!
    Oh, keep us in Thy love,
    And guide us to that happy land
    Of perfect rest above.

337. Oh, how He loves!

MISS. MARIANNE NUNN, 1813.

HUBERT P. MAIN, by per.

1. One there is a-bove all oth-ers, Oh, how He loves! His is love be-
2. 'Tis e - ter - nal life to know Him, Oh, how He loves! Think, oh, think how
3. All your sins shall be for-giv - en, Oh, how He loves! Backward shall your

yond a broth-er's, Oh, how He loves! Earth - ly friends may
much we owe Him, Oh, how He loves! With His pre - cious
foes be driv - en, Oh, how He loves! Best of bless - ings

fail or leave us, One day soothe, the next day grieve us,
blood He-bought us, In the wil - der - ness He sought us,
He'll pro-vide you, Nought but good shall e'er be-tide you,

But this Friend will ne'er de - ceive us, Oh, how He loves!
To His fold He safe - ly brought us, Oh, how He loves!
Safe to glo - ry He will guide you, Oh, how He loves!

338.   Homeward Bound.

Rev. W. F. WARREN.   C. S. HARRINGTON.

1. Out on an o-cean all boundless we ride, We're homeward bound, homeward bound,

Tossed on the waves of a rough, rest-less tide, We're homeward bound, homeward bound.

Far from the safe, qui-et har-bor we've rode, Seeking our Father's ce-les-tial a-bode;

Prom-ise of which on us each He bestowed, We're homeward bound, homeward bound.

2 Wildly the storm sweeps us on as it roars,
    We're homeward bound,
  Look! yonder lie the bright heavenly shores,
    We're homeward bound.
  Steady, O pilot! stand firm at the wheel,
  Steady! we soon shall outweather the gale;
  O, how we fly 'neath the loud-creaking sail,
    We're homeward bound.

3 Into the harbor of heaven now we glide,
    We're home at last;
  Softly we drift on its bright silver tide,
    We're home at last.
  Glory to God! all our dangers are o'er,
  We stand secure on the glorified shore,
  Glory to God! we will shout evermore.
    We're home at last.

Hark! ten thousand Harps.—Concluded.

heaven re - joi-ces;   Je-sus reigns, the God of love;   See,   He sits on yonder throne;

See, He sits   on yonder throne;

Je-sus rules the world alone.   Hal-le-lu-jah, Hal-le - lu-jah, Hal-le - lu - jah! A - men.

Je -sus rules   the world a-lone.

2 King of glory! reign for ever—
　Thine an everlasting crown;
Nothing, from Thy love, shall sever
　Those whom Thou hast made Thine own;—
Happy objects of Thy grace,
Destined to behold Thy face.

3 Saviour! hasten Thine appearing;
　Bring, oh, bring the glorious day,
When, the awful summons hearing,
　Heaven and earth shall pass away;—
Then, with golden harps, we'll sing,—
"Glory, glory to our King!"

342.   Jesus, still Lead on.
(FATHERLAND.)
Western Melody.

1. Jesus, still lead on, Till our rest be won; And, although the way be cheerless, We will follow
2. If the way be drear, If the foe be near, Let not faithless fears o'ertake us, Let not faith and
3. Jesus, still lead on, Till our rest be won; Heav'nly Leader, still direct us, Still support, con-

calm and fearless; Guide us by Thy hand To our Father-land, To our Father-land.
hope forsake us; For, thro' many a foe, To our home we go, To our home we go.
sole, protect us, Till we safe-ly stand In our Father-land, In our Father-land. A - men.

343. Lessons from the Cross.

H. BONAR.

(STABAT MATER.)

Unknown.

1. From the cross the blood is fall-ing, And to us a voice is call-ing,

Like a trum-pet sil - ver-clear. 'Tis the voice an - nounc-ing par - don.

It is fin-ished, is its bur-den, Par-don to the far and near.

2 *God is Love;*—we read the writing
Traced so deeply in the smiting
Of the glorious Surety there,
God is Light;—we see it beaming,
Like a heavenly dayspring gleaming,
So divinely sweet and fair.

3 Cross of shame, yet tree of glory,
Round thee winds the one great story
Of this ever-changing earth;
Centre of the true and holy,
Grave of human sin and folly,
Source of nature's second birth.

344. STABAT MATER.

1 Near the cross was Mary weeping,
There her mournful station keeping,
Gazing on her dying Son:
There in speechless anguish groaning,
Yearning, trembling, sighing, moaning,
Through her soul the sword had gone.

2 What He for His people suffered,
Stripes, and scoffs, and insults offered,

His fond mother saw the whole:
Never from the scene retiring,
Till He bowed His head expiring,
And to God breathed out His soul.

3 But we have no need to borrow
Motives from the mother's sorrow,
At our Saviour's cross to mourn.
'Twas our sins brought Him from heaven,
These the cruel nails had driven:
All His griefs for us were borne.

4 When no eye its pity gave us,
When there was no arm to save us,
He His love and power displayed:
By His stripes He wrought our healing,
By His death, our life revealing,
He for us the ransom paid.

5 Jesus, may Thy love constrain us,
That from sin we may refrain us,
In Thy griefs may deeply grieve:
Thee our best affections giving,
To Thy glory ever living,
May we in Thy glory live.

Jacoponi da Todi. (—1306.)
Tr. by Rev. J. W. Alexander, 1842, ab.

345. God, that madest Earth and Heaven.

HEBER & WHATELY.　　　　　　　　　　　　　THOS. B. SOUTHGATE.

1. God, that mad - est earth and heav - en, Dark - ness and light;
2. Guard us wak - ing, guard us sleep - ing, And, when we die,

Who the day for toil hast giv - en, For rest the night: May Thine an - gel
May we in Thy might-y keep - ing, All peaceful lie: When the last dread

guards de - fend us, Slum - ber sweet Thy mer - cy send us,
trump shall wake us, Do not Thou, O Lord, for - sake us,

Ho - ly dreams and hopes at - tend us, This live - long night.
But to reign in glo - ry take us With Thee on high.　A - men.

346.   **An Evening Prayer.**

Unknown.   (LAST BEAM.)

1. Fad - ing, still fad - ing, the last beam is shining; Fa - ther in heav - en, the
2. Fa - ther in heav - en, oh, hear when we call! Hear, for Christ's sake, who is

day is de-clining; Safe - ty and in-no-cence fly with the light, Temp-ta - tion and
Sav-iour of all; Fee - ble and fainting, we trust in Thy might; In doubting and

dan - ger walk forth with the night; From the fall of the shade till the
dark - ness, Thy love be our light; Let us sleep on Thy breast while the

morning bells chime, Shield me from danger, save me from crime, Fa-ther, have mer - cy,
night ta - per burns, Wake in Thine arms when morn-ing re-turns. Fa-ther, &c.

214

An Evening Prayer.—Concluded.

Fa-ther, have mer - cy, Fa-ther, have mer-cy thro' Je-sus Christ our Lord. *A-men.*

347. Ten thousand times ten thousand.

H. ALFORD.   (ALFORD.)   J. B. DYKES.

1. Ten thousand times ten thousand, In sparkling raiment bright, The armies of the

ransomed saints Throng up the steeps of light: 'Tis finished, all is finished, Their fight with

death and sin: Fling o - pen wide the gold - en gates, And let the victors in. *Amen.*

2 What rush of hallelujahs
  Fills all the earth and sky!
What ringing of a thousand harps
  Bespeaks the triumph nigh!
O day, for which creation
  And all its tribes were made!
O joy, for all its former woes
  A thousand-fold repaid!

3 O then what raptured greetings
  On Canaan's happy shore,
What knitting severed friendships up,
  Where partings are no more!
Then eyes with joy shall sparkle,
  That brimmed with tears of late,
Orphans no longer fatherless,
  Nor widows desolate.

848.
Joyfully! Joyfully!

W. HUNTER, D.D.

Rev. A. D. MERRILL.

1. Joy-ful-ly, joy-ful-ly onward I move, Bound for the land of bright spirits a-bove;
An-gel-ic chor-is-ters sing as I come, "Joy-ful-ly, joy-ful-ly haste to thy home."
Soon, with my pilgrimage end-ed be-low, Home to that land of delight will I go;
Pilgrim and stranger no more shall I roam, Joy-ful-ly, joy-ful-ly rest-ing at home.

2 Friends fondly cherished have passed on before,
Waiting, they watch me approaching the shore;
Singing to cheer me through death's chilling gloom,
"Joyfully, joyfully, haste to thy home."
Sounds of sweet melody fall on my ear;
Harps of the blessed, your voices I hear!
Rings with the harmony heaven's high dome!
"Joyfully, joyfully, haste to thy home."

3 Death, with thy weapons of war lay me low,
Strike, King of terrors, I fear not the blow,
Jesus hath broken the bars of the tomb:
Joyfully, joyfully, will I go home.
Bright will the morn of eternity dawn,
Death shall be banished, his sceptre be gone,
Joyfully, then shall I witness his doom:
Joyfully, joyfully, safely at home.

349. Sweet is the Work, my God, my King.

I. WATTS.　　　　　　　(MIGDOL.)　　　　　　LOWELL MASON, 1839.

1. Sweet is the work, my God, my King, To praise Thy name, give thanks, and sing; To show Thy love by morning
2. Sweet is the day of sa-cred rest; No mortal care shall seize my breast; Oh, may my heart in tune be
3. My heart shall triumph in my Lord, And bless His works and bless His word; Thy works of grace, how bright they

light; And talk of all Thy truth at night.
found, Like David's harp of sol-emn sound!
shine! How deep Thy counsels! how divine!

4 Lord, I shall share a glorious part,
　When grace hath well refined my heart,
　And fresh supplies of joy are shed,
　Like holy oil to cheer my head.

5 Then shall I see, and hear, and know
　All I desired or wished below;
　And every power find sweet employ,
　In that eternal world of joy.

350. While with Ceaseless Course the Sun.

J. NEWTON.　　　　　　(BENEVENTO.)　　　　　　S. WEBBE.

1. While, with ceaseless course, the sun Hasted thro' the former year, Many souls their race have run,
D. S.—We a lit-tle longer wait,

FINE.

Nev-er more to meet us here: Fixed in an e-ter-nal state, They have done with all below;
But how lit-tle none can know.

D. S.

2 As the winged arrow flies
　Speedily the mark to find;
　As the lightning from the skies
　Darts, and leaves no trace behind,
　Swiftly thus our fleeting days
　Bear us down life's rapid stream;
　Upward, Lord, our spirits raise,
　All below is but a dream.

3 Thanks for mercies past receive;
　Pardon of our sins renew;
　Teach us henceforth how to live,
　With eternity in view:
　Bless Thy word to young and old;
　Fill us with a Saviour's love;
　And, when life's short tale is told,
　May we dwell with Thee above!

217

Index to Subjects.

Index to Subjects.—Concluded.

Metrical Index.

GENERAL INDEX.

Titles in Small Caps—First Lines in Roman.

General Index.

www.ingramcontent.com/pod-product-compliance
Lightning Source LLC
Chambersburg PA
CBHW030327270326
41926CB00010B/1533